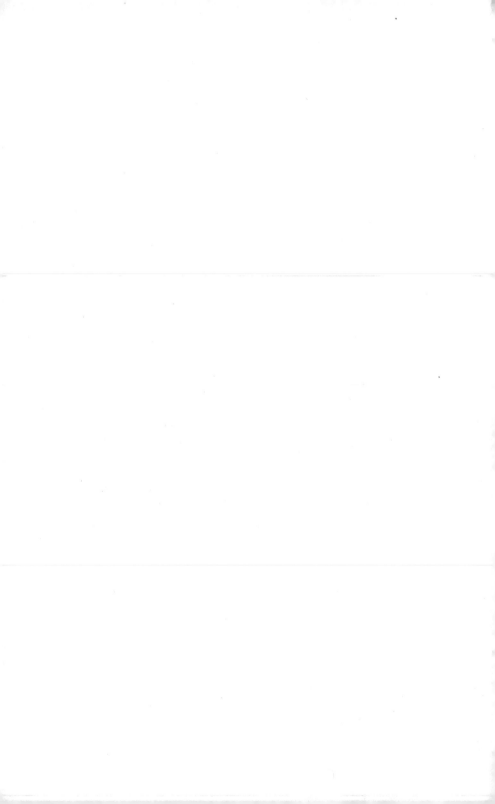

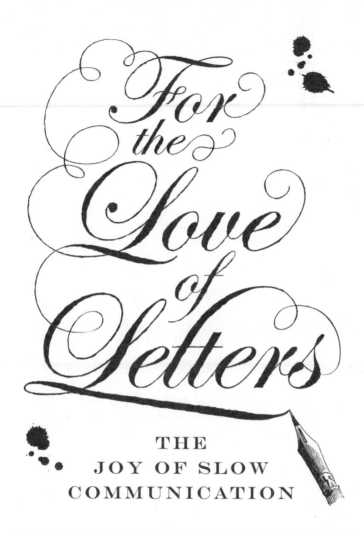

For the Love of Letters

THE JOY OF SLOW COMMUNICATION

JOHN O'CONNELL

MARBLE ARCH PRESS

MARBLE ARCH PRESS

Marble Arch Press
1230 Avenue of the Americas
New York, NY 10020

Copyright © 2012 by John O'Connell
Originally published in Great Britain in 2012 by Short Books

First Marble Arch Press trade paperback edition January 2013

Marble Arch Press is a publishing collaboration between Short Books,
UK, and Atria Books, US.

Marble Arch Press and colophon are trademarks of Short Books.

For information about special discounts for bulk purchases, please
contact Simon & Schuster Special Sales at 1-866-506-1949
or business@simonandschuster.com

Manufactured in the United States of America

10 9 8 7 6 5 4 3 2 1

Library of Congress Cataloging-in-Publication Data

ISBN 978-1-4767-1880-4
ISBN 978-1-4767-1881-1 (ebook)

For Cathy, Scarlett and Molly, and
in memory of Beryl Patricia Earl
(1932–2011)

Contents

Part 1

Of Basildon Bondage

How to Start

I'm sitting at the kitchen table. It's 9.15pm and the children are asleep.

A standard lamp behind my left shoulder casts the only light. In front of me is a sheet of Smythson's paper. In my right hand I am holding the Mont Blanc fountain pen my wife bought me about ten years ago. I have filled it with Burgundy Red ink from one of those beautiful, shoe-shaped Mont Blanc ink bottles, the ones with the 'last-drop' reservoir at the front.

I'm going to write a letter to a friend I haven't been in touch with for a while; a friend who, after my mother died six months ago, sent me the most fantastic letter, an account of her experience of her own mother's death. It stood out because it was so helpful and sensitive, and because it was an actual, old-fashioned letter she had clearly taken trouble over.

To my shame I replied by email, too consumed with organising the funeral to do anything more considered. But now the letter is going to get a proper reply.

At least, I hope it is.

I'm nervous. What if I screw it up? This paper is expensive. I can't afford to waste it. Maybe I should do a rough first? But then I'd be tempted to revise, and re-revise, and gradually I'd lose the spontaneity, the in-the-momentness I want the letter to have.

Or is that what I want? Aren't there any number of possible things a letter can have, and be?

I shut my eyes. Summon the will.

Stop worrying. Just get on with it.

I want the letter to feel 'written', not scrappy, so must follow the same procedure as when I'm trying to write fiction: coax my brain into a state where it isn't sensitive to distraction.

Silence and solitude are vital. Samuel Richardson: 'The pen is jealous of company. It expects, as I may say, to engross the writer's whole self.'

The nib touches the paper. And instinctively I follow the old formula: address in top right-hand corner; date just beneath it on the left-hand side. My writing looks weird. I hand-write so infrequently these days that I've developed a graphic stammer – my brain's way of registering its impatience and bemusement.

What are you doing? Send a sodding email. I haven't got all night.

It's ridiculous, really. Before the advent of email I wrote letters all the time, maybe ten a week. I was useless on the phone, but in a letter I could say what I meant – seem fluent and purposeful. And when replies came I could file them away in padded envelopes in my wooden 'letters chest': secret treasure – unless their authors had kept fair copies, the letters were the only proof of their existence. They had no footprint. If I destroyed them, no-one would know they had ever been written.

When did I stop writing letters? It can't have been *that* long ago – can it?

I'm 40 now. I started using email regularly in 1997, the year I bought my first PC. Like everyone else, I was seduced by the sheer ease of it; persuaded that email must, because it asked so little of me, have the evolutionary edge on snail mail. Only in the last year, as texting and Twitter – which ask even less of me – threatened to supersede email, have I started to wonder why I stopped writing letters when I enjoyed it so much.

All of us, as we age, harp on about what we think we've lost. Concrete things like looks, abstract things like innocence and direction. Nostalgia gives credence to this negative view of the world, coating the past in a treacly goo that's one part glaze and two parts barrier cream.

Without realising it, I'd consigned letter-writing to the 'lost' box. But – a thought-flash – *that didn't mean it had to stay there*. If I wanted to, and if I was quick enough, I could retrieve it before the goo-spreaders got to it, as I did with vinyl records.

I don't listen to vinyl records all the time. CDs and MP3s are fine and serve a purpose. But when played on reasonable-quality kit, vinyl sounds a lot better than sharp, tinny CDs, and loads better than MP3s, which are so compressed that over half the 'sound picture' is missing. More and more people are realising this: sales of vinyl increased by 14% in 2010 according to Nielsen SoundScan.

Yes, it's less *convenient* to listen to vinyl. You can't carry it around with you. It's prone to scratching and warping. But the benefits are colossal.

Before I became a letters bore, I was a vinyl bore. Frequently, after a dinner party, my wife would have to take me to one side. 'Will you stop going on about "analogue warmth"?'

'I'll try,' I said. 'But people have to understand: we've been sold this idea of progress and it's... *wrong*. Just because you develop a new thing, it doesn't mean earlier versions of that thing have to become obsolete. Especially when the earlier versions had their own unique qualities.'

Just as the vinyl experience is enhanced by buying good-quality records – 180g releases from Simply Vinyl, say, or the Vinyl Factory – letter-writing is more enjoyable if you use proper paper.

My hunt for the right sort of paper to write this letter on took most of the day. It started in WH Smith, the source of all my younger self's stationery needs. But as Morrissey didn't quite sing: *Has the world changed or has Smith's changed?* Amid the riot of tacky branding – everything seemed to be Hello Kitty- or JLS-themed – it was hard to find no-nonsense writing paper.

The best Smith's could manage was Three Candlesticks watermarked A4 'correspondence paper' by John Dickinson, the venerable British company which owns the Basildon Bond brand.

Now, I quite like Three Candlesticks. For mass-produced, not-extortionately-priced paper, it's pretty

good. Leagues ahead of pseudo-posh Basildon Bond
– so christened after a John Dickinson director holi-
dayed at the Palladian country house Basildon Park
in Berkshire and thought: hang on a sec...

However, I left WH Smith paperless, certain I
could do better.

Next stop: Paperchase.

Once, I loved Paperchase. Now I think: never
was a shop more aptly named. Because where is
it? Where's the bloody paper?? I can see gifts and
toys and boxes and files and bags. I can see birthday
cards, I can see *note* cards. But I don't want those.

Ah, here it is. Paper. Oh, sorry, no – it's a 'letter
set'. With birdcages on.

Over there – what is it? Paper! It's paper! Oh
happy day!! Well, sort of. It's 'spectrascope rainbow'
paper, good for nothing except laying before your
children with some scissors and glue.

By the time I've found something resembling
Actual Writing Paper I Might Want To Buy, I'm so
angry with Paperchase I can't bring myself to give
them my money.

And so to Smythson's.

You know Smythson's. It's the world-famous,
aeons-old stationery shop on London's Bond Street
where Prime Minister David Cameron's wife
Samantha works designing bags – yes, yes: it's a

stationery shop but it also sells bags, do keep up – and teeny-tiny pale blue lambskin-bound note-books (cost: £30) with cute words or phrases like 'Snogs' and 'Follow Your Dreams' on the front.

I didn't go there to buy a £30 notebook. I went there, frustrated by its high-street not-really-com-petitors, to buy the finest writing paper money can buy. Not much of it, obviously, because I haven't got much money and Smythson's is ridiculously expensive.

I wandered around, staring at all the *stuff*, trying to look harmless and low-key. But within seconds I was intercepted by a beautiful Japanese woman who asked if she could help me.

When I said that she could, she led me towards the back of the shop, to a small glass-fronted cabinet containing plain, unpersonalised writing paper. The paper, she explained, was available in cream and Nile Blue as well as white. It was milled exclusively for Smythson's, bore its 'own distinctive Smythson's watermark' and came in a dandy Nile Blue box. Cost: £14.50 for 50 sheets of 10" x 8".

The starburst in my chest felt like love.

'What about envelopes?' asked the beautiful Japanese woman.

'I suppose,' I said. 'Are they expensive?'

'£15 for 25. But they fit the paper perfectly.'

'You'd expect them to, wouldn't you? For £15.'

The beautiful Japanese woman packed them carefully in a Nile Blue drawstring bag. It took a little while – there was lots of business with tissue paper and tape – so she was obliged to make small talk while I waited.

'I don't like all this rain,' she said.

'No. Though we are in a drought, aren't we? So, the more rain the better. I suppose.'

Smiling, the woman held up the bag for me to snatch, which I did before racing across the shop floor and out into the soaking street.

I Hope You Are Well

It sounds random and crazed, this obsessing over a letter, this blithe buying of expensive paper from a shop it had never even occurred to me to visit before.

But there was a trigger.

The previous week I'd been clearing out my mother's flat when I found a box file containing all my letters home from boarding school. I was nine and at prep school when I scratched out the first with my brand-new Osmiroid fountain pen, fourteen when I agonised over the last.

I was surprised my mother had kept the letters. She wasn't generally sentimental about the past, even her children's. Perhaps archiving zeal got the better of her? It usually did; her genealogy research filled her spare bedroom and took us an entire day to pack up.

(In case this sounds contradictory, I should explain that she made an exception for letters from distant relatives who lived over 100 years ago.)

I never kept any of the letters my mother sent me at school, but then I wouldn't have done: it's a child's prerogative to live in the present and treat everything as ephemeral. My earliest saved letters are from sixth-form girlfriends, all two and a half of them (the girlfriends, not the letters).

The letters-home-from-school, though... There were hundreds of them! The envelopes were small and frequently manilla, and the stamp value rose in pleasing half-penny increments until 1984 when the coin was abolished. We moved around a lot during this period, so the addresses too betray time as well as place: 1981 – Newbury, Berkshire; 1982 – Market Drayton, Shropshire; 1983 – Stockport, Cheshire...

I don't think I'm exaggerating when I say that they're the worst letters ever written.

Do you know the word 'phatic'? It's the word linguistics experts use to describe speech which establishes a mood of sociability rather than conveys information. When someone talks and you go 'Hmmm, mmmm', you're being phatic – displaying a sort of primal animal sympathy; saying, in effect, 'Keep going, I'm still here', even though mentally you may be a hundred miles away.

My letters home *aren't even phatic*. They do not establish a mood of sociability. They establish a mood of... Christ, I don't know. *You* decide.

Dear Mummy and Daddy,

I hope you are well, I am fine. Greenwood got done for talking last night. He has a new Tintin book, Tintin in the Congo. There was supposed to be rugby yesterday but the ground was to (sic) hard so it was canceled (sic).

Today the film is Star Trek: The Motion Picture.

Lots of love,
John

Dear Mummy, Daddy and Alexandra

I hope you are well. I'ts (sic) been a very long and hectic week! Greenwood was sick on my bed last night, and Matron got very angry! Also, Matron found eggs in my hair. Goodness knows how?! So, all our brushes were put in disinfectant and a couple of other boys and my hair was foaming in 'Derbac' for the next 24 hours! All in one short week!!

Today the film is Battle Beyond The Stars.

Lots of love,
John

The context of their composition goes some way towards explaining these letters' distracted strangeness. Letter Writing Hour was on Sunday mornings, you see; after mass but before Scouts – the magical moment when we escaped into the woods behind the school to light unsupervised bonfires, listen to illegal Walkmans and 'purify' water from puddles using special socks ordered from army catalogues.

Letter Writing Hour was a temporal antechamber to mayhem. The whole point of it, as far as we were concerned, was that it would soon end and release us into the world of untamed nature and/or dysentery. But a letter had to be produced in the course of it, to which end it was rigorously policed.

When you'd finished writing, you waved your letter at pale, paunchy Mr Gubbins and he mooched over to check it for neatness (no crossings-out), length (at least two paragraphs long), style (address in top right-hand corner, 'lots of love' at the end because for God's sake they were *still your parents* even if you never saw them) and, most important of all, content.

So no, these weren't the world's best letters. But the

effect reading them had on me was confounding and vertiginous. Within minutes I was in tears, bunched fist crammed into my mouth like the child I once was. Partly this was a grief response; but it was also a response to their materiality – their state-of-physical-beingness, as opposed to an email's state-of-digital-nothingness.

The journalist Catherine Field put it well when she wrote in the *New York Times* on February 3, 2011: 'A good handwritten letter is a creative act, and not just because it is a visual and tactile pleasure. It is a deliberate act of exposure, a form of vulnerability, because handwriting opens a window on the soul in a way that cyber-communication can never do.'

For all their virtues, emails are mere pixels on a screen. Printed out, they lack even the mechanical quirks of typewritten text: the too-forceful exclamation marks, the Jagged Edge-style raised 't's'. I can't locate my mother within hers without making a crude speculative leap – imagining her hunched over her laptop, frowning as her right index finger seeks out the ampersand key.

Reading my letters set me wondering: why do we write letters? How do letters work? What would a really good letter, the kind of letter I would want to receive, look like?

It made me think, with the irrational sentimentality of the bereaved: *wouldn't it be brilliant if we all wrote really rich, detailed letters to each other, which we kept as physical artefacts to pass on to future generations?*

Because to answer my own question, the reason we write letters is the main reason we write anything: to convert the chaos of our lives into solid, time-locked narrative.

The writing of narrative, any kind of narrative, helps us stay sane by convincing us that we are stable, autonomous individuals moving smoothly through the world. That letters' intended recipients are other people roots us in what we now call a social network. (We don't generally write letters to ourselves. A letter to yourself is a diary.)

With letters, as opposed to emails, which are obviously sent and received instantaneously, correspondents are unable to reply immediately; so the results are (or should be) longer, more careful, more persuasive – more conscious of being written outwards, towards someone, indeed 'into' someone in anticipation of a particular type of response.

Does a good letter have a distinct compositional form? Should decent letter-writers be familiar with classic epistolary theory as set down in the nine epistles of the Attic rhetorician Isocrates? Of course not; although it's interesting that rhetorical models that existed in the fourth century BC still influence written communication today: among the Isocratean letters are letters of patronage, letters supplying character references, letters asking favours, letters offering counsel...

In the Middle Ages, letter-writing was taught as an adjunct of rhetoric. The earliest preserved Western medieval letter-writing manual was created at the end of the eleventh century by a Benedictine monk called Alberic. Teaching *ars dictaminis* – the rhetorical art of letter-writing – it was designed for scribes who needed to learn how to write legal documents.

Most *artes dictandi* were brief; designed to be read aloud to the recipient rather than silently and in private; and contained five sections:

1 SALUTATIO: a formal greeting. *Warmest salutations!*

2 CAPTATIO BENEVOLENTIAE: an attempt to snare the reader's attention and win him over. *I have been thinking about you a lot recently.*

3 NARRATIO: the background to the request or demand. *I don't know if you heard, but I recently lost a lot of money in a dispute over an ox.*

4 PETITIO: the request or demand. *Please could*

you lend me some before bailiffs torch my dwelling-house?

5 CONCLUSIO: the formal ending, including a blessing and a date. *I remain your humble servant, etc. May God rain mercy upon you. June 5th, 1322.*

Over the next few hundred years – very, *very* broadly – letters become more flexible in their uses, more personal, and more elegant. And as we head into the Renaissance, the *salutatio* and *captatio bene-volentiae* bits expand while the other bits contract. The guy everyone wants to imitate is Cicero. His letters to Atticus, Quintus and Brutus, discovered in the Chapter Library in Verona in 1345, possess reflective subtlety as well as formal beauty.

Then there's Erasmus. He's important because he introduced the idea that letters could have all kinds of functions and be written in all sorts of ways. The goal for him was *copia* or 'abundant expression' – transforming a commonplace formula such as 'your letter pleased me greatly' by finding exactly the right verbal variation. (He was working in Latin, obviously.)

Erasmus tells his students to increase their linguistic aptitude by amassing examples from authors they like: 'One should collect a vast supply...[and] provide oneself with a varied equipment, and, as Quintilian remarks, heap up riches so that we find we have a wealth of words to hand whenever we require it.'

Ostentation is vulgar, says Erasmus, referring specifically to the habit in the *salutatio* of comparing the addressee to the sun, a shining lamp, a flower, etc. In style, the best letters should resemble not shouting in a theatre but whispering in a corner with a friend.

The classical model falls away in the seventeenth century as more people start writing in English. During the eighteenth and nineteenth centuries, thousands of manuals are published so that ladies and gentlemen of breeding can use the appropriate epistolary mode at the appropriate time.

Does this result in lots of good letters? Or just lots of boringly similar letters? A bit of both, I suspect, depending on which manual you were fortunate/unfortunate enough to own.

One manual-cum-anthology from 1868, *The Art of Letter-Writing*, advises: 'Write as you speak, write just what you have to say, write exactly the things you feel, exactly the words you would say if your correspondent were sitting by you – in short ... write "what comes uppermost"; so your letters will be true, fresh, life-like and interesting.' A letter,

it says, should be 'a picture of your thoughts, interesting to your correspondent in exactly the same
proportion as he or she is interested in yourself or
your concerns'.

I like this a lot. The idea that a good letter should
mimic conversation – should represent in some way
speech perfected – feels right to me, as it probably
does to you.

An obvious retort to this, however, is: *if that's
what you want letters to be, aren't you better off writing
an email? They're right on the cusp between the written
and the spoken and satisfy all your demands for flex-
ibity and informality.*

It's a valid point. And I must stress here that I don't
hate email at all. I use it all the time. But in some ways
it's *too* informal. People don't read it properly and
they receive too much of it. Email isn't momentous;
it's commonplace. As for being 'on the cusp' between
the spoken and the written, it's truer to say it falls
between the gaps in ways that aren't always helpful.

What about the business of *actually getting letters
to people*? It's a crucial one, not least because the
ability to send and receive letters quickly expedites

stylistic change by lowering people's tolerance for staid old formulas.

Of the many things the Romans did for us, one of the most useful was invent a postal system: first the *vehiculatio* (wagons and mules, basically), then the *cursus publicus*, a sort of state-run courier service created by Emperor Augustus whose main purpose was gathering information about an enemy's troop movements.

At this point letters were written with a pen on papyrus, wood or parchment, though wax and a stylus were used for erasable messages on tablets. Some of these, dating from AD 100, were found at Vindolanda on the Stanegate frontier road south of Hadrian's Wall.

Fast-forward to Britain in the twelfth century and the origins of our postal service are visible through the fog; though at this stage the Royal Mail was a private channel between the monarch and local government. Royal messengers to Surrey, Sussex and Middlesex were allowed one day for travel and paid twopence. Those travelling to further-flung destinations like Cumberland and Wales received 20 pence for a journey lasting eight days. By 1271 the volume of royal correspondence had increased to the point where 32lb of wax was being used each week to seal the strips of parchment on which letters were inscribed.

The poet Thomas Hoccleve (c1368–1426) worked for 30 years without promotion as a scribe in the Privy Seal Office. The job, which required a lot of stooping and squinting, damaged his back and his eyesight. As for the money – well... he whinges about the indignities of it all in his poem 'The Regement of Princes':

VI marc, yeerly, and no more than that
ffadir, to me, me thynketh is full lyte
Consideryng, how that I am nat
In housboundrye, lerned worth a mite.

Most of the letters Hoccleve worked on would have gone to sheriffs – the king's agents at a local level and the men responsible for collecting revenue and captaining the local army. Private epistolary correspondence was possible only for those who could afford to pay servants to be postmen. The aristocratic Paston family, whose letters spanning the years 1422 to 1509 are a vital source of information about medieval life, used a family retainer to carry letters between London and their base in Norwich.

Henry VIII established a master of the posts in 1516. In 1635, Charles I made the Royal Mail available to the general public. Dorothy Osborne, daughter of the last royalist to remain fighting for Charles, courted her husband Sir William Temple with witty letters which she mostly sent using private carriers. She did this to stop her family, who disapproved of the match, from intercepting them. When she moved to London in the early 1650s she experimented with the Royal Mail, but a letter of June 1654 suggests service was patchy:

> *Why doe you say I failed you indeed I did not Jane is my witnesse she carryed my letter to the White-hart by Snt Jameses, and twas a very long one too.*

In 1660, under Charles II, came major upgrading: the establishment of a General Post Office presided over by a postmaster general; a postmark for tracking speed of delivery; a system of six 'post roads' devoted to mail; and a weekly postal service from London to Dublin and Edinburgh.

The network expanded thanks to entrepreneurs like Ralph Allen, Postmaster at Bath, who introduced a system of signing for letters upon receipt and the so-called 'cross-post', whereby letters no longer had to travel via London. And lo! England's roads vibrated to the rumble of mail coaches. The first to carry the black-and-scarlet Royal Mail livery appeared in 1784. Mail coaches were drawn by four horses and could carry four passengers inside and a few more outside with the driver. A guard stood at the back where the mail was kept.

The results seem to have been satisfactory. 'The Post Office is a wonderful establishment,' remarks Jane Fairfax in Jane Austen's *Emma*. 'The regularity and despatch of it! If one thinks of all that it has to do, and all that it does so well, it is really astonishing!' John Knightley replies: 'It is certainly very well regulated.'

By this time there were several deliveries a day within London. Just after dawn one October morning in 1816, the year of *Emma*'s publication, Keats sat down and wrote his sonnet 'On First Looking Into Chapman's Homer'. He put a copy into the post in Southwark and it reached its recipient Charles Cowden Clarke by ten o'clock that morning.

The most peculiar feature from our viewpoint is that postage was paid not by the sender but by the recipient on delivery. Cost was worked out based on distance travelled and the number of sheets of paper used. It was common for the poor to go without food to pay for the receipt of a letter.

One way of keeping costs down was so-called 'cross-writing' – not to be confused with Allen's cross-post. In cross-writing, rather than use a new clean page to continue a letter, you turned it over and wrote over the existing text at a right angle. In *Emma*, again, Miss Bates refers to a cross-written letter she has received from her niece Jane Fairfax: 'My mother often wonders that I can make it out so well.'

(In his *Eight or Nine Wise Words About Letter-Writing*, published in 1890, Lewis Carroll cautions against cross-writing because 'cross-writing makes cross reading'. He recommends sticking the stamp and writing the address on the envelope right at the beginning to avoid the 'wildly-scrawled signature – the hastily-fastened envelope, which comes open in the post – the address, a mere hieroglyphic'.)

Envelopes hadn't been invented yet. Letters were folded and sealed with a wax stamp, and would probably still have been written on hand-made paper: the mass production of paper began in 1801 with the invention of the Fourdrinier machine, which made a continuous roll rather than individual sheets.

Hand-made paper was/is produced using a mould – a wire screen in a wooden frame. Fibrous slurry settles and dries on the mould before being turned out on to a felt sheet made of animal fur. The ribbing and other marks visible on the paper are indentations from the mould. Lines running sideways are 'laid lines'; impressions made by the wires holding the sideways wires together are 'chain lines'. Watermarks occur where a design has been deliberately woven into the wire.

What sort of pens did people use? Jane Austen wrote her letters and novels using a goose quill. The feather's hollow shaft, the *calamus*, acts as a reservoir for the ink, which flows to the tip by capillary action. Quills remained popular until the 1820s, when they were superseded by the metal pen.

Jane's Hampshire home at Chawton in Hampshire is now the Jane Austen House Museum. Visit it – you should – and marvel at the tiny twelve-sided walnut table where she sat, hunched over small sheets specially chosen so that they could easily be put away or covered if someone entered unexpectedly.

Her sloped writing box is in the John Ritblat Gallery in the British Library, in a glass case alongside her spectacles (tiny wire frames, like a doll's spectacles) and two cancelled chapters of *Persuasion*.

I popped in and had a look at it earlier this morning – I'm writing this in the British Library. Of course its aura is overwhelming, amplified by the signs of wear and tear and the gentle purple lighting. After I had paid my respects I stood a little way away, in the Beatles lyrics section, and watched successive waves of Janeites fighting the urge to genuflect.

Writing boxes were the laptops or tablets of the nineteenth century. Jane Austen's, thought to have been bought for her by her father in December 1794, has a leather writing slope, space for two inkwells and compartments for pens, stamps, sealing wax, etc. Lockable, secret drawers were a common feature.

Boxes were mostly used for letting-writing – they could be moved easily to the warmest or most private part of the house – though obviously Austen wrote her novels on hers, as did Anthony Trollope, who had a 'travelling' desk which he used on the train. But I digress...

In 1838 the Great Western Railway opened, linking London with the south-west and west of England and most of Wales. Within ten years trains had replaced mail coaches in all but the most remote areas. Volume was an issue as well as speed: the introduction of the pre-paid Penny Post in May 1840 saw 112,000 stamped letters posted, nearly four times the normal number. Finally, the post was for everyone.

Yet the Penny Post had its critics. And their criticisms will sound strangely familiar.

'I suppose there has never been so much letter-writing in the world as is going on today, and much of it is good writing, as the papers show,' sighs AG Gardiner in his late-Victorian essay 'On Letter-Writing', before reaching the devastating conclusion that 'in the great sense letter-writing is no doubt a lost art. It was killed by the Penny Post and modern hurry.'

The essay is persuasive and worth quoting at length:

When Madame de Sévigné, Cowper, Horace Walpole, Byron, Lamb, and the Carlyles wrote their immortal letters, the world was a leisurely place where there was time to indulge in the luxury of writing to your friends. And the cost of franking a letter made that letter a serious affair. If you could only send a letter once in a month or six months, and then at heavy expense, it became a matter of first-rate consequence. The poor, of course, couldn't enjoy the luxury of letter-writing at all. De Quincey tells us how the dalesmen of Lakeland a century ago used to dodge the postal charges. The letter that came by stage coach was received at the door by the poor mother, who glanced at the superscription, saw from a certain agreed sign on it that Tom or Jim was well, and handed it back to the carrier unopened. In those days a letter was an event.

Now when you can send a letter half round the

globe for a penny, and when the postman calls half a dozen times a day, few of us take letter-writing seriously. Carlyle saw that the advent of the Penny Post would kill the letter by making it cheap. 'I shall send a penny letter next time,' he wrote to his mother when the cheap postage was about to come in, and he foretold that people would not bother to write good letters when they could send them for next to nothing. He was right, and the telegraph, the telephone, and the postcard have completed the destruction of the art of letter-writing. It is the difficulty or the scarcity of a thing that makes it treasured. If diamonds were as plentiful as pebbles we shouldn't stoop to pick them up.

So, then — as Kingsley Amis once moaned about the expansion of access to higher education, 'more means worse': or does it?. It's true *in a sense* that scarce commodities are more valuable than plentiful ones. But really, the only way you're going to kill something by making it cheap is if you lower its material quality to the point where it stops functioning. More people writing letters for less money isn't going to diminish the value of letters *per se* — unless you think letters sent by poor people lack value.

To be honest, every time a change was made to the way people wrote, sent or received letters there was a fuss. Take Mulready 'stationery letter sheets' – envelopes you could write on, a bit like aerograms. Their launch in 1840 coincided with the Penny Post's, but while the stamp was a huge success, the public *hated* Mulreadies, particularly the elaborate illustration of Britannia and a reclining lion (by painter William Mulready, hence the name) that festooned them.

After only six days the postal reformer Rowland Hill wrote in his journal: 'I fear we shall have to substitute some other stamp for that design by Mulready... The public have shown their disregard and even distaste for beauty.'

Two months later, Mulreadies were withdrawn.

Then there's the pillar post box, introduced to Britain in September 1853 by Anthony 'travelling writing desk' Trollope in his capacity as a Post Office surveyor. Trollope had spotted pillar-boxes in France and been impressed. But in his 1869 novel *He Knew He Was Right* we find spinster aunt Jemima Stanbury expressing what must have been a widespread suspicion:

[She] had not the faintest belief that any letter put into one of them would ever reach its destination.

She could not understand why people should not walk with their letters to a respectable post-office instead of chucking them into an iron stump, — as she called it — out in the middle of the street with no-one to look after it.

Chattily Substantial

Was there a Golden Age of Letters? The literary critic Frank Kermode thought so; also that its span was wide — it lasted, he thought, from 1700 to 1918, and to his mind was extended rather than truncated by the Penny Post. If you're going to be nit-pickingly canonical, the Golden Age begins with Queen Anne's coronation in 1702, stretches a little way into Victoria's reign and centres on a First Division of seven or eight epistolers — broadly the writers Gardiner name-checks in his essay.

The letter-as-narrative-art-form was forged in the same furnace as the novel and the mass of bold political writing that inspired the Augustan period's history-textbook soubriquet 'the Age of Satire'. As the critic George Saintsbury puts it in *A Letter Book* (1922), a 'middle style' neither grand nor vulgar had evolved in line with a desire for letters to be chattily substantial rather than straightforwardly formal:

You gave the news of the day, if your corre-
spondent was not likely to know it; the news
of the place, especially if you were living in a
University town or a Cathedral city. If you had
read a book you very often criticised it: if you had
been to any kind of entertainment you reported on
it, etc, etc.

Underpinning all this – and it sounds para-
doxical, I know – was a belief that a letter was a
performance, a turn on the trapeze of your intel-
lect that had to be worth the money or you were
cheating the recipient.

Broadly, the stars of the show were:

JONATHAN SWIFT (1667–1745)

Anglo-Irish essayist, novelist, pamphleteer who
became Dean of St Patrick's Cathedral in Dublin.
His most famous letters – to two close female
friends, Esther Johnson and her companion Rebecca
Dingley, addressed collectively as 'MD' – form the
Journal to Stella (1710). Johnson was the fatherless
daughter of a servant at Moor Park, the estate of
the diplomat Sir William Temple for whom Swift
worked as secretary. Swift met her when she was
eight and became her tutor and mentor. His relationship with Johnson is mysterious and has kept

scholars guessing. Were they married? If so, was the relationship ever consummated? The Stella letters – intimate, gossipy and very, very silly – are written in a 'little language' which mimics the speech of small children, eg 'I expect a Rettle vely soon; & that MD is vely werr, and so Nite dee MD' ('I expect a letter very soon, and that my dears are very well, and so night dear my dears').

It was always thought that prudish eighteenth-century editors had censored the correspondence. But digital analysis of the original letters has shown that Swift crossed out the rude bits himself as part of a three-way game he played with the women. As Dr Abigail Williams, the editor of a recent Cambridge University Press edition of Swift's collected works, explains, the women 'needed to undress the text before they could fully enjoy it'. Swift's disguising of endearments created a 'secret code of intimacy' they were supposed to crack.

Swift is famous also for his grandstanding, rather self-conscious letters to his friends Alexander Pope, John Gay and Tory leader Bolingbroke. But the Stella letters – and the later 'Vanessa' letters to another mysterious Esther, Esther Vanhomrigh – are more interesting. George Saintsbury puts his finger on it when he calls them 'absolutely genuine and free from the slightest taint of writing for publication': 'Perhaps appreciating or not appreciating the "little language" is a matter very largely of personal constitution, and the failure to appreciate it is (like colour-blindness or other physical deficiencies) a thing to be sorry for, not to condemn.'

WILLIAM COWPER (1731–1800)

Poet and hymn-writer Cowper isn't discussed much nowadays, but he gave us the phrases 'Variety's the spice of life' and 'God moves in a mysterious way/ His wonders to perform'. Although he found solace in hardcore evangelical Christianity, his certainty that he was doomed to eternal damnation eventually became all-consuming and he spent his last years waiting mutely for God to do his worst.

That such a man should be one of the sharpest, most casually hilarious letter-writers of his time is strange indeed. But it happens to be true, even if, as Saintsbury observes, 'the matter which these letters have to chronicle is often the very smallest of small beer'. On and on Cowper blathers about the height of chairs, the condition of a fish someone has bought for him, the length of his candlesticks, whether the fashion for wigs will lead to people cutting off their own legs and substituting artificial ones...

As one critic has it, Cowper 'sought in the infinitesimal a cure for the disease of brooding on the infinite'. Writing these letters helped enormously to alleviate his depression.

Cowper wore a bag or cap on his bald head and only green- or brown-coloured clothes. He loved cuckoo clocks but disliked travel. As a young man he studied law and wrote light prose for a magazine called *The Connoisseur*. But at 32 he had his first breakdown and tried to hang himself. (He blamed his bad nerves on an incident in his childhood where a skull thrown at him by a gravedigger rolled up and struck him on the leg.) He lived in Huntingdon with a couple called the Unwins, but when the Reverend Morley Unwin was killed after a fall from a horse, he and Mrs Unwin moved to Olney in Buckinghamshire to be near their friend the Reverend John Newton, a former slave-trader who had seen the error of his ways and found God. Actually, Newton sounds like a psychopath – he had a reputation for 'preaching people mad' and was eventually hounded out of the parish – but he became one of Cowper's two main correspondents, the other being his cousin Lady Hesketh.

At Olney, he worked in a summerhouse the size of a sedan chair, producing big poems like 'The Task' and smaller ones like 'Verses Written at Bath on Finding the Heel of a Shoe' and 'On the Death of Mrs Throckmorton's Bullfinch'. He was modest about his abilities, declaring: 'I have no more right to the name of poet than a maker of mouse-traps has to that of an engineer.' To stave off depression he became a jack-of-all-trades: the point was to fill up the day with distractions. 'The necessity of amusement,' he wrote to Mrs Unwin's clergyman son, 'makes me sometimes write verses; it made me a carpenter, a birdcage maker, a gardener, and has lately taught me to draw':

> *Alas, what can I do with my wit? I have not enough to do great things with, and these little things are so fugitive that, while a man catches at the subject, he is only filling his hand with smoke. I must do with it as I do with my linnet;*[1] *I keep him for the most part in a cage, but now and then set open the door, that he may whisk about the room a little, and then shut him up again.*

Attacks of religious melancholy crippled him in his final years, and on his deathbed, asked how he felt, he replied: 'I feel unutterable despair.'

Cowper hated the idea of his letters being published or even read after his death by anyone except their intended recipients. For this reason he was careful to destroy all but business

---

1 A mainly brown and grey finch with a reddish breast and forehead.

correspondence: 'I account it a point of delicacy not to leave behind me when I die, such bundles of [my friends'] communications as I otherwise should, for the inspection of I know not whom; and as I deal with theirs, for the very same reason, I most heartily wish them all to deal with mine.'

SAMUEL RICHARDSON (1689–1761)

The earliest novels were epistolary, and the daddy of them all is former printer Richardson's *Pamela: or Virtue Rewarded* (1740), written when its author was 51.[2] He had lofty ambitions for its form as well as its content:

> *I thought the story, if written in an easy and natural manner, suitably to the simplicity of it, might possibly introduce a new species of writing, that might possibly turn young people into a course of reading different from the pomp and parade of romance-writing, and dismissing the improbable and marvellous, with which novels generally abound, might tend to promote the cause of religion and virtue.*

---

2 Epistolary novels had been around a while by this point: Aphra Behn's *Love-Letters Between a Nobleman and His Sister* appeared in 1684. Pierre Choderlos de Laclos's much loved *Les liaisons dangereuses* was published relatively late in the day, in 1782.

The epistolary method, thought Richardson, added drama as well as authenticity. Instead of an omniscient narrator telling you what was going on, letters supplied multiple viewpoints: 'We need not insist on the evident superiority of this method to the dry narrative; where the novelist moves at his own dull pace to the end of his chapter and book, interweaving impertinent digressions, for fear the reader's patience should be exhausted.'[3]

As a youth Richardson was renowned for his letter-writing skills and would help girls of his acquaintance reply to love letters: 'I have been directed to chide, and even repulse, when an offence was either taken or given, at the very time that the heart of the chider or repulser was open before me, overflowing with esteem and affect.'

The inspiration for *Pamela* was a moral primer in the form of letters which Richardson was commissioned to write by his friends Charles Rivington and John Osborn. Intended for 'the lower classes of people', it was regarded by Richardson as hack-work but became a huge success when it finally appeared, shortly after *Pamela*, under the pithy title *Letters Written to and for Particular Friends, on the Most Important Occasions. Directing not only the*

---

3 This is a dig at his rival Henry Fielding's non-epistolary novel *Tom Jones* (1749). Fielding had disliked *Pamela* and parodied it in his novel *Shamela* (1741).

*Requisite Style and Forms to be Observed in writing
Familiar Letters; but how to Think and Act Justly and
Prudently, in the Common Concerns of Human Life.*

Richardson's masterpiece, the ginormous epistolary novel *Clarissa; or the History of a Young Lady*,
appeared in 1748.

LADY MARY WORTLEY MONTAGU (1689–1762)

Astonishing proto-feminist aristo socialite who
'stole' an education, teaching herself Latin in the
library of her father's mansion, Thoresby Hall in
Nottinghamshire. By fourteen she had written
two books of poems, an epistolary novel and a
prose-and-verse romance modelled on Aphra
Behn's *Voyage to the Isle of Love*. Her father wanted
her to marry the awesomely named Clotworthy
Skeffington, heir to an Irish peerage, but she refused
and eloped instead with the man she loved, Edward
Wortley Montagu.[4] They married in August 1712,
drifting thereafter into the orbit of George I and the
Prince of Wales. Her caustic wit – example: 'The
one thing that reconciles me to the fact of being
a woman is the reflexion that it delivers me from
the necessity of being married to one' – won her

---

4 As an MP, Edward Wortley Montagu introduced a Bill to 'secure the
property in books to the rightful owners thereof'. In other words, we
have him to thank for copyright law.

membership of the Kit-Kat Club but made enemies of Alexander Pope (who once declared his love for her) and Horace Walpole (see below), who attacked her 'impudence, avarice and absurdity'.

In 1715 a satirical poem she had written about Caroline, Princess of Wales while recovering from smallpox[5] found its way into circulation. Forced to leave court in disgrace, she accompanied her husband on a trip to Istanbul where the pair remained until 1718. Mary chronicled the period in a series of letters which became known as the Turkish Embassy Letters: frank, graphic descriptions of Islamic and other practices she was able to witness because she was a woman who earned the trust of other women. Her famous account of a bathhouse – I discuss it later – inspired Ingres's 1862 painting *The Turkish Bath*, which shows nude women in a harem.

Aged 69, she boasted that she had not looked into a mirror for eleven years. Once, at the opera, someone commented disapprovingly that her hands were dirty. She replied: 'You should see my feet.'

Her dying words were: 'It has all been most interesting.'

---

5 Smallpox ruined her looks, leaving her with pitted skin and no eyelashes.

HORACE WALPOLE (1717–97)

The 4th Earl of Orford is best remembered for Strawberry Hill, the Gothic folly he built in Twickenham, and the gothic novel *The Castle of Otranto* which he published anonymously, pretending to have found it in the ancient library of a family in the north of England. But his thousands of letters are held by scholars to be more important than either.[6] Although they are self-conscious in the sense that Walpole wrote them with posterity in mind, as accounts of the age, they avoid pomposity and at their best conflate public and private modes in spectacular, addictive fashion. As George Saintsbury remarks:

> *Their style, though recognisable at once, is not a matter so much of phrase as of attitude... He cannot, or at least does not, give a plot of any kind: every letter is a sort of review of the subject – larger or smaller – from the really masterly accounts of the trial of the Jacobite Lords after the 'Forty-five' to the most trivial notices of people going to see 'Strawberry'; of remarkable hands at cards; of Patty Blount[7]... in her autumn years passing his*

---

6 In a letter dated January 28, 1754, Walpole invented the word 'serendipity'.

7 Martha 'Patty' Blount (1690–1762): literary groupie and friend of Alexander Pope.

windows with her gown tucked up because of the rain... There is of course nothing very 'arresting'. Cooking chickens in a sort of picnic with madcap ladies and expecting 'the dish to fly about our ears' is perhaps the most exciting incident of the 16 volumes and seven or eight thousand pages. But everywhere there is interest; and that of a kind that does not stale itself.

Walpole, who never married, was famous for his effeminacy and obsessive love of his mother. But if he was gay, he seems to have repressed it. His contemporaries regarded him as asexual; an unkind political opponent called him a 'hermaphrodite horse'. His closest friends were lesbians like the sculptor Anne Seymour Damer, to whom he left Strawberry Hill after his death.

Lots of people hated him and found him affected and silly. But then Walpole found himself affected and silly, as he wrote to Sir Horace Mann:

Pray, my dear child, don't compliment me any more upon my learning; there is nobody so superficial. Except a little history, a little poetry, a little painting, and some divinity, I know nothing. How should I? I, who have always lived in the big busy world; who lie a-bed all the morning, calling it morning as long as you please; who sup in company; who have played at pharaoh half my life, and now at loo till two and three in the morning; who have always loved pleasure; haunted auctions – in short, who don't know so much astronomy as would carry me to Knightsbridge, nor more physic than a physician, nor in short anything that is called science.

Saintsbury's summing-up is more measured:

An unkind critic with a turn for rather obvious epigram might say that the man's nature was so artificial that his artifice seems natural. If so, all the more credit to him as an artificer.

JANE AUSTEN (1775–1817)

Clever woman. Wrote some novels. And a lot of letters, mostly to her sister Cassandra who – would you believe it? – burned the bulk of them and doctored the rest to remove unseemly references to physical ailments and other private business. The letters are light and fluffy rather than momentous: Great Thoughts About Pressing Issues Of The Day are thin on the ground.

Another oft-hurled criticism is that they are snobbish and bitchy – *cf* the critic HW Garrod's notorious 1928 dismissal of them as 'a desert of trivialities punctuated by occasional oases of clever malice'. This seems plain wrong when you consider what a supreme ironist Austen was. A statement like 'You know how interesting the purchase of a spongecake is to me' (from a letter dated June 15, 1808) shouldn't be taken literally; and of course letters between siblings as close as Jane and Cassandra have a particularly complex tone – a tone that's almost a code in itself and therefore perilously easy to misjudge.

The Golden Age isn't the whole story. Over the last hundred or so years there have been: the Mitfords (yawn), Bertrand Russell, Ernest Hemingway, *et al*; though some of the best regarded are diminished by their reliance on vaudevillian slapstick. Think of the self-consciously 'outrageous' correspondence of Kingsley Amis and Philip Larkin, where the wit is almost eclipsed by blunt misogyny and sour racism.

Perhaps that's unfair. Amis's letters are frequently hilarious, and you could argue that the hermetically sealed world they inhabit permits even offensive excursions: they were a private game, like

Swift's Stella letters, and we should be careful how we judge them.

The Amis/Larkin letters are certainly unbuttoned. But unbuttoned, with its suggestion of trousers being loosened after a large lunch, is not the same as honest. For that you need to go to Larkin's letters to his long-time lover and confidante Monica Jones, which dwell, Cowper-like, on the small stuff: noisy neighbours, disagreeable food, what he got (or rather didn't get) for Christmas – 'A laundry bag (asked for), a 10/6 book token, a second-hand tie, & a pair of expanding cufflinks enamelled in blue with large "P"s in cursive script on them. That's all, that's all, that's all, that's all. Shan't get very fat on all that, eh?'

Personal aside: for all that Larkin's letters are brilliant, if I'm going to spend time in the company of a depressive poet I'd sooner it was Edward Thomas, whose more tangible depression was stoked by the pressures of real life (marriage, kids, bills) rather than by misanthropy. His final letter to his wife Helen, written a few days before his death at the Battle of Arras on April 9, 1917, is beautiful:

Still not a thrush, but many blackbirds. My dear, you must not ask me to say much more. I know that you must say much more because you feel much.

> *But I, you see, must not feel anything. I am just as it were tunnelling underground and something in my subconsciousness directs me not to think of the sun. At the end of the tunnel there is the sun.*

Who else is good? Virginia Woolf, VS Naipaul (I'm thinking of his letters to his father), Arthur Conan Doyle (I'm thinking of his letters to his mother), Samuel Beckett. Of WB Yeats's letters to his muse and platonic love Maud Gonne few survive; but hers to him, which we have, tell the story of their thwarted alliance. The Irish activist's sign-off letter to Yeats as she prepared to marry, was carried around by the poet and almost crumpled into illegibility: 'Friend of mine *au revoir*. I shall go over to Ireland in a couple of months, if you care to see me I shall be so glad & you will find I think that I am just the same woman you have always known, marriage won't change me I think at all...'

Here are some personal favourites, suggested in a spirit of give-it-a-go geniality rather than prescriptive arrogance:

ISAIAH BERLIN (1909–1997)

They're not to everyone's taste, the letters of the twentieth century's greatest liberal intellectual. A notorious *Guardian* review by AN Wilson said they were 'not worth the effort required of them': 'There is not one which comes anywhere near being a good letter, and nearly all of them are thunderingly boring.' Really? Surely the pleasure lies in their remorseless, egotistical maximalism. Yes, they are rambling and overlong – many were spoken into a dictaphone and transcribed by his secretary – but that's part of their charm (even if this book disapproves finally of such a practice). At the end of one epic we get as a PS, 'I cannot bear to read through all this: I hope it is not too endlessly discursive & thinly buttered.' Well, since you put it like that... Bursts of self-doubt where he calls himself 'superficial, worthless, glaringly shallow' soften you up for the poisonous, throwaway jibes – Greta Garbo is 'dumb', Einstein has 'the inhumanity of a child'. But then Berlin was, in Michael Oakeshott's brilliant phrase, a 'Paganini of ideas' who quoted from memory in his scholarly work, improving others' words to make them more resonant. What do you expect? Humility? (See also: historian Hugh Trevor-Roper's letters to the art critic Bernard Berenson.)

PENELOPE FITZGERALD (1916–2000)

Late-starting novelist, poet, essayist, etc – she was first published at 58. Her lean novels, like *Offshore* which won the Booker in 1979, explore the uncertain connection between art and life. Her letters, remarkable for their neat italic handwriting, rarely joined up, do this too, though many are missing, lost when her houseboat sank in 1963. Fitzgerald kept her writing hidden from friends, and what's fascinating is how ordinary the letters feel – they don't glow with literariness; they cover the years when she was working at *Punch* and teaching and raising her children. But there's a tension between the domestic business ('It's so awful, I've lost my glasses!') and what you know was going on in another bit of her brain, the bit that wrote the books. The letters are exuberant and often hilarious. They notice everything, even the wardrobe malfunctions of Eurovision entrants: 'Sandie Shaw looked frightful in ostrich-effect feathers...'

ANTON CHEKHOV (1860–1904)

Chekhov's letters (not strictly twentieth century, I know, but they might as well be) are clear and clean and careful, full of plain-speaking wisdom as befits a man who hated pomposity and refused to cloak his own emptiness with 'other people's intellectual rags'. The letters cover his early years of struggle as he tries to balance hack writing with work as a doctor. A letter of praise from the novelist Dmitri Grigorovich means 'more than any diploma'. Highlights are the act-by-act account of the disastrous-sounding first night of Ivanov and the reactive travelogue inspired by his visit to the Siberian convict island of Sakhalin in 1890, 'a place of intolerable sufferings'. As a hypochondriac, I'm intrigued by his account of the cholera epidemic in 1892 – Chekhov treated it by giving tannin enemas. And of course he becomes ill himself, with tuberculosis, which necessitates months of invalid exile in Nice. To Alexander Chekhov: 'A will must be draw up, without delay, so that you won't be able to grab all my property.' The letters between Chekhov and his actress wife Olga Knipper ('my exquisite little missis', 'my little crocodile' etc), for whom he created the part of Masha in Three Sisters, have a desperate, lonely air. She pursues her career in Moscow while he is ill in Yalta. He is always telling her to stop moping and being cross. His last letter, written from Badenweiler four days before he died on July 2, 1904, was to his only sister Maria Chekhova. Chekhov's final observation: 'You don't see a single decently dressed German woman, the lack of taste is depressing.'

EVELYN WAUGH (1903–1966)

Waugh wrote to John Betjeman on June 11, 1946: 'There is nothing painful about writing letters provided one writes nothing else. I have given up work of all kind.' The crotchety novelist hated the telephone and made it known that he should be written to instead. If someone called with a request he refused to acknowledge it until they put it in writing. His most famous letters are to Nancy Mitford when she was living in Paris, but my Mitford allergy makes it hard for me to enjoy them. Waugh wrote letters in the morning when he was sober, his diary at night when he wasn't. The letters are joke machines, built to amuse. Their comic method is manic exaggeration and an accretion of short, childlike sentences: 'I have got fat again'; 'Here is my new novel. I hope you will like it'; 'I am sad and bored and need your company.' The early ones, when he is teaching and struggling with his writing, are angsty and self-deprecating. As he ages he becomes harsher, nastier, more bilious. Religious zeal intrudes in annoying ways, as in his letter to George Orwell complaining about the absence of the Church in *Nineteen Eighty-Four*: 'I believe it is inextinguishable.' His letters to his son Auberon at school are wonderful, full of good advice, sympathetic but wary of the pitfalls of full-scale anarchy: 'There is no superiority in shirking things and doing things badly.' Sometimes the letters are so saturated in irony that it's hard to work out what, if anything, Waugh is trying to achieve beyond amusing himself. This, to T W Gadd, who had sent him a poem, sounds just like Charles Ryder's father in *Brideshead Revisited*: 'Pray do not suppose that my inability to enjoy modern art is a source of pride to me. I deplore it. Nor is it the fruit of affluent circumstances. I know many richer & better educated than myself, who rejoice in Picasso.'

WINSTON AND CLEMENTINE CHURCHILL (1874–1965 & 1885–1977)

The Churchills wrote to each other constantly – a dialogue stretching all the way from 1908, four years after they first met at a ball, to 1964, the year before Winston's death. As their daughter Mary Soames notes, the extraordinary thing about these letters is their 'spontaneity and naturalness'. Reading them feels transgressive because public figures, especially wartime prime ministers, are not supposed to be so gushy and silly and sign off with little drawings of pugs and kittens. Many of the letters were written when they were both in the same house (Chartwell) at the same time: Clementine was not good in argument, and would retreat to her room to unjumble her thoughts on paper. The letters show how, against the odds, and despite colossal differences, relationships can be held together by love, kindness and mutual respect. I like Winston's first letter from Chartwell, sent on April 17, 1924 and full of child-like glee at the new house: 'I drink champagne at all

meals & buckets of claret & soda in between, & the
cuisine tho' simple is excellent.'

Part 2

Letters and Life

How They Fit Together

Letters shape and define lives. They also encapsulate them much more effectively than biography because they show rather than tell us what a person was like.

This process starts at the very beginning. We may not write letters when we're babies, but we are written to, and about; and our parents are written to, being too tired to write themselves.

Confronted with a newborn, even the most prolific correspondents fall silent. Rebecca West typically wrote several long letters each day, managing over 10,000 in the course of her lifetime; but her output dwindled to nothing during the period in 1914 when she was packed off to the seaside by her lover HG Wells to have their baby.

Even Winston and Clementine Churchill's relentless correspondence falters in July 1909, around the time Clementine gives birth to their first child Diana, aka – in the letters' private language – 'the PK'.

Admittedly, modern childbirth is the sort of occasion where email comes into its own. Off goes the announcement to everyone in your address book – a blockade of terse euphemism. *Mother and baby both fine... kept in for observation... perhaps a trifle pale...*

But the problem with sending emails is that you get emails back. I forgot to print out the replies to our email announcing the birth of our eldest child before accidentally wiping them from the hard drive. No-one could say they deserved this, even if a lot of them were variations on a theme of 'Brilliant!!!!! Hope we see you all soon!' – so not exactly written with posterity in mind.

The mass of websites devoted to telling people what to say in cards and letters suggests either a massive collective awkwardness when it comes to celebrating significant moments in life or (more likely) a massive collective failure of imagination.

One called healinglovenotes.com has some particularly odd advice: 'New parents believe sincerely that their baby is the best, brightest and most beautiful ever born. A note to celebrate a birth should tell them they're right!'

Healinglovenotes' recommended phrases are frankly emetic.

It's a miracle! You must be so happy and proud. What a lovely family you make!

What a beautiful baby! I'm guessing he/she has you wrapped around those perfect little fingers already.

The bar for letters to new parents would seem to have been set high – by Jane Austen in the letter she sent her brother Frank on the birth of his son, also called Frank, in July 1809. It takes the form of a poem written in rhyming couplets.

My dearest Frank, I wish you joy
Of Mary's safety with a boy,
Whose birth has given little pain,
Compared with that of Mary Jane.

Okay, so it's doggerel. But you know, Paul McCartney wrote 'Hey Jude' *and* 'Ob-La-Di, Ob-La-Da'. Genius is inconsistent.

One of the most moving birthday letters is by Dorothy Wordsworth, sister of the more famous William, written to her friend Lady Beaumont, wife of the painter and patron of the arts Sir George Beaumont, who co-founded the National Gallery.

Look carefully and you'll see that, while it has an air of spontaneity, it's carefully structured to accommodate all the necessary nuggets. To make sense of it you need to know that William's wife Mary has just given birth to the third of the couple's five children. The previous two were John (born June 18, 1803) and Dora (August 16, 1804). The as-yet-unnamed subject of this letter was born on June 15, 1806.

My dear Friend

You will rejoice with us in my sister's safety, and the birth of a son. There was something peculiarly affecting to us in the time and manner of this child's coming into the world. It was like the very same thing over again which happened three years ago; for on the 18th of June, on such another morning, after such a clear and starlight night, the birds singing in the orchard in full assembly as on this 15th, the young swallows chirping in the self-same nest at the chamber window, the rose-trees rich with roses in the garden, the sun shining on the mountains, the air still and balmy, — on such a morning was Johnny born, and all our first feelings were revived at the birth of his brother two hours later in the day, and three days earlier in the month; and I fancied that I felt a double rushing-in of love for it, when I saw the child, as if I had both what had been the first-born infant John's share of love to give it, and its own.

We said it was to be called William at first, but we have since had many discussions and doubts about the name; and [the poet Robert] Southey, who was here this morning, is decided against William; he would keep the father's name distinct, and not have two William Wordsworths. It never struck us in this way; but we have another objection which does not go beyond our own household and our own particular friends, ie that my brother is always called William among us, and it will create great confusion, and we cannot endure giving up the sound of a name which, applied to him, is so dear to us. In the case of Dorothy there is often much confusion; but it is not so bad as it would be in this case, and besides, if it were only equally confusing, the inconvenience would be doubled.

Other business follows, much of it concerned with a visit Lady Beaumont is shortly to make to the Wordsworths' house at Grasmere ('I hope you will find the inn tolerably comfortable...'); then Dorothy returns to the Name Problem in a postscript:

*I have expressed myself obscurely about our objec-
tions to calling the child by William's name. I
meant that we should not like to call him but as we
have been used to do. I could not change William for
brother, in speaking familiarly; and his wife could
not endure to call him Mr Wordsworth. Dorothy [ie
the baby's elder sister] is in ecstasies whenever she
sees her little brother, and she talks about him not
only the day through but in her dreams at night,
'Baby, baby!'*

After all this, the child was eventually called
Thomas.

It feels gratuitous, a piling-on of sorrow, to
mention here that Thomas died aged six and a
half, from measles. But I must, because the death
inspired William Wordsworth to write a beautiful
letter to Southey on December 2, 1812:

*For myself dear Southey I dare not say in what state
of mind I am; I loved the Boy with the utmost love
of which my soul is capable, and he is taken from
me — yet in the agony of my spirit in surrendering
such a treasure I feel a thousand times richer than if
I had never possessed it.*

The language is rich, exalted. To us today it

almost seems too much — so unlike the language we use when we email each other, and a world away from the bubble of instant nothing that is a tweet.

But written down it works, especially as a counterpoint to his sister's letter. Because Dorothy's letter, with its meticulous itemising of dates and circumstances, feels like an experiment in slowing down time, or at least in highlighting the lag between clock time and the rate at which we register change. It wants to hold on to and explore the moment because the moment may not (and, in this case, does not) end the way anyone wants it to.

Children and the Idea of Letters

What do today's children make of letters? Very little, you might think. But you would be wrong. Their parents may not write many, but because children are constantly encountering letters or the idea of them in books, they have no awareness of them as obsolete.

The continuing popularity of a book like Janet and Allan Ahlberg's ingenious, interactive *The Jolly Postman*, in which post is delivered to an array of characters from fairy tales, proves the point. Here, wittily personalised letters for each character (a writ issued to the Big Bad Wolf by lawyers who want him out of Grandma's cottage; Goldilocks' 'sorry' letter to the Three Bears) are tucked into envelopes between the pages. The letter is at once part of the story and independent of it, which to a child is a thrilling idea as it suggests the characters are too.

As I write this, my daughter Scarlett is reading Penelope Farmer's 1969 novel *Charlotte Sometimes*, in which Charlotte communicates by letter with Clare, the girl she becomes when she mysteriously travels back to 1918. Charlotte and Clare never meet – the letters, written in an exercise book hidden in the leg of a bed, are the only link between them, the only means Charlotte has of shoring up her dissolving identity.

Which is appropriate, because that's what letters do: fix people in time the way hyposulfite fixes a photographic image. At badsey.net, a website celebrating the history of the Worcestershire town of Badsey, you can find letters written by children who attended Badsey Council School in the early 1930s. Even though the children were obviously forced to write them as part of an exercise – the writing is uncannily neat and the spelling perfect – the letters are revealing about who these children were and how they lived. They were, in the main, poor, with home lives that didn't leave a lot of time for anything except work. Here is nine-year-old Hilary Crane, writing on April 11, 1933:

Dear Sir

I live in Badsey which is in the Vale of Evesham. My father is a market gardener. I go to Badsey Council School. We have fourteen in our family. My father is pulling onions and my mother is tying them. My sister and I go to help to pick plums in the summer also gooseberries and currants which are black and red. Father also has a lot of asparagus and daffodils. He sends his produce to Evesham market which he takes in a horse and cart. We also send gellies to market which my sister and I help to pick. We pick beans and peas in the summer for my father. My mother and my big sister help to do all the things that I do. I tie onions and pick daffodils which are grown in the ground.

I remain,
Yours truly
Hilary Crane (aged 9)

Why would the children have been asked to present this information in the form of a letter? Because while a diary is an equally effective time capsule, a letter is oriented outwards, towards a person or context (in this case, the Future).

Letter-writing is still taught in British schools. In fact, it's a required element within the Key Stage 2 National Literacy Strategy. 'Children are expected to learn how to write letters, notes and messages,' says the blurb. 'They have to be aware of different styles of writing, the use of formal and informal letters, and to select style and vocabulary appropriate for the intended reader.'

Letter-writing is still deemed 'an essential skill':

Despite the prevalence of emails and text messages, everyone has to write letters at some point. Letters of complaint, job applications, thank you letters, letters requesting changes or making suggestions — the list goes on and on. Encouraging children to write letters from an early age will improve their communication, social and handwriting skills, and teach them what they need to know about writing and structuring letters.

Filial Duty

I'm not sure there have ever been rules, even in the most austere writing manuals, governing how children write to each other. You'd have to be a real sour square not to agree that anything goes. The way children should write to adults, however, was something the Victorians got characteristically worked up about. *The Handbook of Letter-Writing* from 1861 has this to say on the subject:

> *Children away from home, in the excitement of new scenes and fresh acquaintances, may for a time forget and neglect their parents; but moments must recur reminding them of their affectionate solicitude, and in trouble and affliction making them yearn for a sympathy they may then only in its absence thoroughly appreciate, and it is at such times that a letter relieves the heart of the writer and moves that of*

the parent. Children should, however, accustom themselves to write regularly to their parents, and they should express themselves in the same easy, cheerful way that they would do in speaking at home. The only rule we think it necessary to lay down is the propriety of preserving a due regard to the relationship in which the writers are placed to each other. A father, when writing to his son, should preserve his superiority by a gentle degree of authority, and a son should never lose sight of the manner in which he can best express his sense of filial duty.

There follow some sample letters, the most bizarre aspect of which is their specificity. Here, for example, is a boy of ten writing to his father in the Welsh countryside:

Will you try to bring me a cormorant to stuff? Or, if it would cost too much to have it stuffed, bring me a wild duck's nest, with the eggs in it.

I may have been a weird child, but I never asked my father for a cormorant.

I like the sample letter from father to son at school supplied in *The Gentlemen's Letter Writer* (1890):

My Dear Son

I am delighted to hear of your progress, and send you a little remittance of pocket-money, to prove to you that I am ever ready to give encouragement where it is deserved. You must always bear in mind that upon your career at school much of your future life must depend. To waste the precious hours of youth is to make preparation for a useless and dishonourable old age...

We laugh at this now, as if it is how the Past was. Even at the time, though, few parents would have sent a letter like this. These manuals were for people who didn't write many letters and were deeply unconfident about the process. Compare 'real-world' ones from roughly the same period and the contrast couldn't be clearer.

This is from the Scottish journalist Sir William Robertson Nicoll to his seven-year-old daughter Mildred:

Hotel St James, Paris, October, 1905

Dearer Mildred,

So you have begun to write reviews! Very good indeed. Always praise your book.

This is a nice big white city with very broad streets. There are a great many toy shops in it. I am going out to look at them. Perhaps I will buy a dolly for myself. I think I would like a dolly. It would be nice company for me — would it not?

Your very loving, Popsy Wopsy

In the early 1840s William Makepeace Thackeray's daughters Anny and Harriet lived with his parents while their mother Isabella was incapacitated with post-natal depression. The letters he sent them during this period are written in large print and festooned with drawings.

I have nothing to send my dearest Anny but a little picture: — The picture is of some little girls I saw going to church and one of them I thought was like Anny.

Well, this is all I have to say, for there is no time, because the person is waiting who is going to take this. God bless the little girl to whom he is going to take it, and her little sister. Do you know their names and that their papa loves them?

As the girls enter their late teens, the tone is sweet and intimate, but more satirical.

Royal Hotel, Sheffield, 1857

This comes rather late for Valentine's Day. It is copied from 6 mugs in my sitting room at the horrible inn at Halifax. This is a byootiful Inn. I have the gayest parlour looking over three smoky streets – a clean snug bedroom – a snug sleep – a pleasant book to read – Colonel and Mrs Forrest came to tea last night after the lecture that's y I didn't write to the girls. I liked them both, she pretty and blonde, he very gentlemanlike. The people for the most part didn't understand a word of the lecture. Old Fogey President of the Institution introduced me & insisted upon toddling into the room with me on his arm. What, is Mr Thackeray infirm? asks Mrs F of her husband. It was old Fogey who was infirm. I had a very pleasant calm day at Fryston, and yesterday for dinner here ate a pheasant, one of a brace which old Mr Milnes insisted on sending to my daughters, though I told him I wasn't going home…

I wish those horrible newspapers would leave my health out. Some day the wolf will come and no one will be frightened. Keep off Wolf for a few months. I want to put my lambs in comfort-shelter.

I am in the 4 volume of Mahon. It amuses me. I have read Cockburn's Memorials, very pleasant too. It is delightful weather and the skeei is blyew through the smoke… Do you smell anything in this ink? It was thick, & I filled the bottle with brandy and soda-water. I have nothing to tell my dawlings but that I am very well busy and cheerful…

Not everyone gets the tone right. Some of Sir Walter Scott's letters to his daughter Sophia seem calculated to vex and distress.

Abbotsford, 30 May, (Very like 30 March in Temperature.) 1813.

My dear Sophia

I am sorry to say that poor Cuddy is no more. He lost the use of his hind legs, so we were obliged to have him shot, out of humanity. This will vex little Anne, but as the animal could never have been of the least use to her, she has the less reason to regret his untimely death; and I will study to give her something that she will like as well, to make amends, namely, a most beautiful peacock and pea-hen, so tame that they come to the porch and feed out of the children's hands…

Scott goes on to report that he has procured some of the hair from the corpse of Charles I, 'cut from the head when his coffin was discovered about a month ago in St George's Chapel at Windsor': 'The hair is a light brown. This is my best news. The worst is that everything is suffering from cold and drought.'

The all-time classic passive-aggressive mother–daughter correspondence is that between Marie de Rubetin-Chantal (1626-96), better known as Madame de Sévigné, and her daughter Françoise-Marguerite, who was obliged to leave Paris for Provence after she married the syphilitic Count of Grignan, who at 37 was only six years younger than his mother-in-law and already had two daughters from his first marriage. Mme de Sévigné had negotiated the union: she wanted her daughter to be a countess. For the next 23 years, Mme de Sévigné wrote to Françoise at least twice a week. She had plenty of time on her hands, having been a professional widow since the death of her husband in a duel fought over a mistress.

The letters were not, however, private in any conventional sense. In the salon society of seventeenth-century France, you shared with your friends both your letters and any replies received. The letters were not mere carriers of news, but works of art whose bogus 'spontaneity' is a crucial part of the performance. (As Mme puts it: 'You know that I have only one pen stroke; thus my letters are quite loose, but that's my style, and perhaps it will have as much of an effect as a more fitted one.')

Face to face, Mme de Sévigné and Françoise did not get on very well. Awareness of this drove Mme de Sévigné to idealise their relationship – to the point of reconfiguring it entirely – in letters that teem with gossip and advice on etiquette.

And did I mention the whining? 'I have had but two letters from you; perhaps a third is on the road; they are my only comfort,' writes Mme – and this before her 'infinitely dear' daughter has even *reached* Provence!

On the subject of letter-writing itself Mme has a lot to say, much of it by way of back-handed compliment:

> The pleasure I take in reading [your letters] is beyond all imagination. If I have in any way contributed to the improvement of your style, I did it in the thought I was labouring for the pleasure of others, not for my own...

Performance Anxiety

Letters are often a performance, then, even when they're pretending to be casual and conversational. My sister and I only started to write to each other in our teens. When she was sixteen and I eighteen, Alex left the school we both attended in Staffordshire and went to live with our much older brother and his wife in London.

The function of Alex's letters to me during this period was to establish a mood of bohemian cool; to say, with matter-of-fact relish: 'Hey, I'm living in a squat/in Italy, going out with an artist/learning to fire-eat/reading novels by Sylvia Townsend Warner.'

Mine to her were less engrossing: 'A new shopping centre opened in Hanley last week! It's called the Potteries Centre and has a glass elevator!!!'

It would never have occurred to me at the time – and if it had I would have denied it – but Alex's letters were gently educating me into an awareness of my limitations; saying: 'Cheer up, you can do this sort of thing too: just stop *worrying* so much.'

Some correspondence between siblings is more explicitly improving. In 1799, when he was just sixteen, Henri-Marie Beyle – better known as Stendhal – left his hated Grenoble for Paris to learn mathematics. He didn't study for long, though. He joined Napoleon's army before working for the imperial household in Italy, Germany and Russia. From 1800 onwards he wrote regularly to Pauline, the favourite, younger sister he had left behind, instructing her on how to live: what to read, when to marry, how to navigate the choppy waters of their family.

The letters are fascinating because, like most Letters By Young People, they are exercises in self-fashioning. As the novelist Adam Thirlwell has written, they are 'memoirs from a time of immaturity'. They educate Pauline, but are also attempts by Stendhal to educate himself, to reassure himself that a clean break from the provinces could be made.

Stendhal's greatest contribution to literature, says Thirlwell, is the idea of the 'performative self' delivered up to the world in prose that is 'theatrically natural'. (Stendhal: 'To have a good epistolary style, you have to write down exactly what you would say to the person if you saw them.') What follows is from his first letter to Pauline, written when he was seventeen and she fifteen:

I hardly know what to say, my dear Pauline, when I reflect that I've gone five whole months without writing to you. I've been thinking I must do so for some time now, but I've had so many things on that I haven't got round to satisfying my desire. To begin with, I want you to write to me every week, without fail; if you don't, I'll scold you; then I want you not to show your letters, or mine, to anybody; when I'm writing from the heart, I don't want to feel trammelled. You can tell me how you're getting on with the piano; whether you're taking dancing lessons… I'm taking dancing lessons from a dancer at the Opéra; his style is completely different from Beler's; since the style I'm learning is the right one and, as such, will sooner or later reach the provinces, my advice is that you prepare for it — you have to bend at each step, and make sure you kick your heels up properly… I advise you to ask grandfather to get La Harpe's Cours de littérature *from Chalvet, who must have a copy. And read it; you may find it a bit boring, but it'll tidy your ideas up and I promise you that you'll reap the rewards later on.*

The Advice Squad

As Stendhal shows, an expansive form like the letter is the perfect medium for counsel. In a letter you can structure an argument, build a case; and, assuming the recipient chooses to file it away, there's a hard copy for ease of future referral.

The 'advice' letter is one of the oldest epistolary genres – think of Seneca's moral letters to Lucilius, the Roman governor of Sicily. There are 124 of them, written in the last two years of Seneca's life when he was travelling in southern Italy. The letters give tips on how to become a better Stoic – Stoicism being Seneca's favoured brand of philosophy – deal with one's slaves and, fascinatingly, conquer asthma:

My ill-health had allowed me a long furlough, when suddenly it resumed the attack. 'What kind of ill-health?' you say. And you surely have a right to ask; for it is true that no kind is unknown to me. But I have been consigned, so to speak, to one special ailment. I do not know why I should call it by its Greek name: for it is well enough described as 'shortness of breath'. Its attack is of very brief duration, like that of a squall at sea; it usually ends within an hour. Who indeed could breathe his last for long?

Seneca's letters are not straightforwardly bossy. They use concrete events like illnesses or voyages as a springboard for a range of seasoned reflections on death, friendship, pleasure, the sanctity of marriage, etc. Whether or not Lucilius took Seneca's advice isn't known. But you would be inclined to, simply because of the open-ended, dialogic nature of the way the advice is expressed.

This is also why Rainer Maria Rilke's *Letters to a Young Poet*, written between 1903 and 1908 to a young man about to enter the German military, are so beguiling and effective. Franz Xaver Kappus was nineteen years old and had written to Rilke (who was only eight years older but already infinitely world-weary) looking for guidance and an expert critique of his verse. He was inspired to send Rilke his work after a chance conversation with the chaplain of the military academy where he was studying, an academy Rilke had attended in his youth, before it became clear that his frail health couldn't stand the pace. Kappus did not want the military career that had been mapped out for him. From Rilke, who had been allowed to continue his studies at home in Prague, he wanted 'sympathetic understanding'.

> *Many weeks went by before an answer came. The letter with its blue seal bore a Paris postmark, weighed heavy in the hand and displayed on the envelope the same clarity, beauty and assurance of hand with which the content itself was written from the first line to the last. And so my regular correspondence with Rainer Maria Rilke began, lasting until 1908 and then gradually petering out because life forced me into domains which the poet's warm, tender and moving concern had precisely wanted to protect me from.*

In the event, Rilke gives Kappus little literary advice: 'Any intention to criticise is too foreign to me,' he says (though in the next paragraph he dismisses the poems as having 'no special nature of their own'). Instead he tells him to be patient and to avoid wasting his time in 'unreal, half-artistic' professions like journalism. Ouch.

The letters are wise, eloquent and helplessly

quotable. Take this:

You are so young, all still lies ahead of you, and I should like to ask you, as best I can, dear Sir, to be patient towards all that is unresolved in your heart and to try to love the questions themselves like locked rooms, like books written in a foreign tongue.

Or this:

Take pleasure in your growth, in which no-one can accompany you, and be kind-hearted towards those you leave behind, and be assured and gentle with them and do not plague them with your doubts or frighten them with your confidence or your joyfulness, which they cannot understand. Look for some kind of simple and loyal way of being together with them which does not necessarily have to alter however much you may change.

The effort Rilke has put into the letters is obvious – you can almost detect a thin film of sweat on them – and he admitted to finding letter-writing hard work. The circumstances had to be absolutely right. As he wrote to Kappus from Rome in October 1903: 'Forgive this dilatoriness – but I do not like writing letters while travelling, because I need more for letter-writing than the most necessary implements: some quiet and solitude and a not too incidental hour.'

Something Rilke says which I particularly love is: 'Do not believe that he who seeks to comfort you lives untroubled among the simple and quiet words that sometimes do you good.' Partly, I take this to mean simply that it's hard to live as you preach. But I think Rilke also means that the hallmark of a good teacher is a (private) lack of confidence in his own wisdom.

(In Rilke's case, the letters to Kappus are a bit of a pose, a conscious assertion of intellectual authority at odds with the desperate, depressed tone of the letters he was writing at the time to his ex-lover and confidante Lou Andreas-Salomé.)

You wonder if another famous set of what academics call 'moral-didactic' letters, Lord Chesterfield's *Letters to His Son on the Art of Becoming a Man of the World and a Gentleman* (1774), would have been more effective if they'd been less strident. Chesterfield's letters fall within a sub-genre – advice letters from fathers to sons – so notorious for its pomposity that Shakespeare parodies it in *Hamlet* in the scene where Polonius gives fatherly counsel to Laertes. The collection, which comprises over 400 letters written between 1737 and 1768 to Lord Chesterfield's illegitimate son Philip, were published by Philip's widow, Eugenia Stanhope, after his death.

And this is the supreme irony, because despite Lord Chesterfield's attempted micro-management of his life, Philip never came close to achieving his father's ambitions for him. He kept his marriage to the low-born Eugenia a secret: only after he died aged 36 from dropsy did Lord Chesterfield discover he had a daughter-in-law and grandchildren. Although he provided for the children, he left Eugenia nothing in his will; hence her decision to sell his letters to Philip to a publisher for the sum of 1,500 guineas.

Reading the letters now, you find yourself cheering Philip on and wondering how any sane person is supposed to react to a letter containing advice like this:

I would heartily wish that you may often be seen to smile, but never heard to laugh while you live. Frequent and loud laughter is the characteristic of folly and ill-manners; it is the manner in which the mob express their silly joy at silly things; and they call it being merry. In my mind there is nothing so illiberal, and so ill-bred, as audible laughter. I am neither of a melancholy nor a cynical disposition, and am as willing and as apt to be pleased as anybody; but I am sure that since I have had the full use of my reason nobody has ever heard me laugh.

From Mother to Child

A still-popular tradition – google it and watch the blogs appear – is mothers writing to their own unborn children.

Often this is called 'legacy' writing: a mother leaves her child a sort of conduct manual to be consulted in the event of her death, the letter form producing a rhetorical effect of intimacy and immediacy. Sometimes it's a single, solitary letter. Sometimes it's a whole book. Lady Sarah Pennington's *An Unfortunate Mother's Advice to Her Absent Daughters* (1762) is a halfway house between letter and book – in the sense that it started as the former but was obliged to become the latter.

Separated from her daughters by their father, Lady Sarah was forbidden even from corresponding with them. Having no other choice, she published the letter she wanted to send, hoping they would hear about it and seek it out. This was a deeply transgressive act – high-born women in the eighteenth century did not publish conduct manuals under their own names – and she felt the impropriety of it keenly: 'Was there any probability that a letter from me would be permitted to reach your hand alone, I should not have chosen this least eligible method of writing to you.'

The letters advise her daughters against reading novels of any sort because they are unrealistic and immoral (though she makes an exception for Goldsmith's *The Vicar of Wakefield*). And she is brutally particular about the girls' education:

> *It is necessary for you to be perfect in the four first Rules of Arithmetic; more you can never have Occasion for, and the Mind should not be burdened with needless Application. Music and Drawing are accomplishments well worth the Trouble of attaining, if your Inclination and Genius lead to either; if not, do not attempt them, for it will be only much Time and great Labour unprofitably thrown away, it being next to impossible to arrive at any Degree of Perfection in those Arts, by the Dint of Perseverance only, if a good Ear, and a native Genius are wanting.*

Elizabeth Joscelin's hugely popular *The Mothers Legacie to her Unborne Childe*, went through eight editions between 1624 and 1684. Her original editor Thomas Goad wrote in his preface to the first published edition that the minute Elizabeth 'first felt her selfe quicke with childe (as then trauelling with death it selfe) she secretly tooke order for the buying a new winding-sheet'.

The manuscript, now in the British Library, is signed in a practised italic hand 'Eliza Joscelin'. It is a small duodecimo volume with trimmed pages measuring 7cm by 12cm and was rebound in blue velvet in the nineteenth century. The text averages six or seven words a line and between 20 and 25 lines per page.

Variations in the size and regularity of the handwriting suggest it was written over a number of sittings. One nineteenth-century editor, Randall Davidson, thought he detected in the final pages 'unmistakable signs of physical difficulty or distress'.

> *Having long, often and earnestly desired of God, that I might bee a mother to one of his children, and the time now drawing on, which I hope hee hath appointed to give thee unto me: It drew mee into a consideration both wherefore I so earnestly desired thee, and (hauing found that the true cause was to make thee happy) how I might compasse [attain] this happinesse for thee.*

I knew it consisted not in honour, wealth, strength of body or friends (though all these are great blessings) therefore it had beene a weake request to desire thee onely for an heire to my fortune. No, I never aimed at so poore an inheritance for thee, as the whole world. Neither would I have begged of God so much pain, as I know I must endure, to haue only possest thee with earthly riches, of which to day thou maist be a great man, to morrow a poor beggar. Nor did an hope to dandle [play with] thy infancy moue mee to desire thee. For I know all the delight a Parent can take in a childe is hony mingled with gall.

Early childcare manuals – the kind that started to appear in the eighteenth century – are chatty and avuncular. This was to signpost that they were for 'lay' readers. We can imagine the smile on Hugh Smith's face when he writes in his *Letters to Married Women* (1792): 'Believe it not when it is insinuated that your bosoms are less charming for having a dear little cherub at your breast.'

In 1838, the American Episcopalian writer Lydia Sigourney published *Letters to Mothers*, a gushy collection of her thoughts on babies: 'As a germ quickened by spring, the infant opens the folding doors of its little heart, and puts forward the thought, the preference, the affection, like filmy radicles, or timid tendrils, seeking where to twine.'

Well, quite. It makes you hanker for a more basic, bracing approach – the sort to be found in the uptight, it-could-only-be-English *Letters To A Mother on the Watchful Care of Her Infant* (1831):

My Dear Madam

The most important subject for your observation in regard to your little infant, after attention to its diet, is the condition of its bowels. And, first of all, let me urgently request you to adopt this rule, daily to inspect its evacuations. Anything short of this, is short of your duty...

In this manner, too, some secrets are discovered, some misdoings are detected. A currant, a bit of apple-peel, a raisin-stone, a gooseberry-seed, &c. observed in the evacuations, has unveiled the mystery of an indisposition unaccountable, and has laid bare proceedings unconfessed before.

Letters of Rebuke

Sometimes advice tips over into correction. And sometimes correction tips over into rebuke.

Anyone can be rude. Anyone can write, 'Dear XXX, Will you please sod off?' The trick is to take all the anger and irritation you feel and sublimate it so that you end up with something like the magisterial put-down Samuel Johnson sent James Macpherson on January 20, 1775. Macpherson was the Scottish writer who claimed to have discovered an epic poem by a third-century bard called Ossian. Johnson doubted its authenticity and believed Macpherson had simply stumbled across some fragments of old Gaelic poetry and used them as the basis for his own weak romance. Macpherson was, said Johnson, 'a mountebank, a liar, and a fraud'.

The pair got into an epistolary slanging match which culminated in Macpherson issuing an injunction and Johnson firing this notorious shot across the bows:

Mr James Macpherson

I received your foolish and impudent note. Whatever insult is offered me I will do my best to repel, and what I cannot do for myself the law will do for me. I will not desist from detecting what I think a cheat, from any fear of the menaces of a Ruffian.

You want me to retract. What shall I retract? I thought your book an imposture from the beginning, I think it upon yet surer reasons an imposture still. For this opinion I give the publick my reasons which I here dare you to refute.

But however I may despise you, I reverence truth and if you can prove the genuineness of the work I will confess it. Your rage I defy, your abilities since your Homer are not so formidable, and what I have heard of your morals disposes me to pay regard not to what you shall say, but to what you can prove.

You may print this if you will.

Sam: Johnson

Just to prove that this tone isn't a male preserve... Katherine Mansfield sent one of the best ever just-go-away-you-worm letters to Princess Elizabeth Bibesco, with whom her husband John Middleton Murry was having an affair. The affair Mansfield could cope with, being a sophisticated

Bloomsbury acolyte. But Bibesco's gauche habit of sending Murry love letters was really too much…

24 March, 1921

Dear Princess Bibesco,

I am afraid you must stop writing these little love letters to my husband while he and I live together. It is one of the things which is not done in our world.

   You are very young. Won't you ask your husband to explain to you the impossibility of such a situation.

   Please do not make me have to write to you again. I do not like scolding people and I simply hate having to teach them manners.

When Lady Hamilton had something solemn to say to her daughter Horatia, she piled on the abuse: 'Look into yourself well, correct yourself of your errors, your caprices, your nonsensical follies, for by your inattention your have forfeited all claims to my future kindness… PS Look on me now as gone from this world.'

   Likewise Queen Charlotte Sophia, of whose fifteen children with George III womanising William was the most troublesome. At 64 he inherited the throne, his two older brothers having died.

But in 1785, when he was twenty, his mother sent him an astonishing letter demolishing his personality:

> *Your reasons for liking and disliking are in general so trifling and frivolous that the best judgement one could form upon them would be that of youthful volatility, but when one knows you to be twenty years of age this very month, this excuse can no longer be made & severer judgements must arise, which can be no less than the want of a good heart, want of understanding, ambition, vanity, wilfullness & an uncommon share of caprice, which imperceptibly will lead you to be what you will be ashamed to hear, a true trifling character, which is the most despicable of all things in the world, & the higher the rank the more it is observed; & it is surprizing that with the proofs you give to the world of your offensive pride you do not feel the necessity of a proper behaviour.*

Here Is the News

Letters have always brought news. And since the dawn of photocopying, the most popular epistolary medium for news has been the round-robin.

It's one of the tragedies of the modern world, the way the round-robin has survived, like some demonic post-apocalyptic cockroach, to become the only kind of letter many people ever send or receive.

This should bother us all. Because the round-robin is an evil waste of time, the opposite of the sort of letter this book has made it its business to celebrate. Why are these smug bulletins from the hearth of the too-comfy middle classes still sent when the big-ticket events they celebrate – pay rises, exotic family holidays – are fast becoming things of the past?

As long as there are children in the world, there are achievements to be boasted about. *Guardian* columnist Simon Hoggart's masterful collection of round-robins contains this gem:

Harry was Jesus in the school Jesus Christ, Superstar. This was the best production I have ever seen, youth or adult. Both boys, especially Harry, were physically and emotionally drained at the end. I was drained too... seeing your son crucified nightly is not an experience I would recommend.

According to etiquette expert Judi James, round-robins are usually sent by people who 'want to lead those idealistic family lives, usually with two children. If you have more children, you're too busy. And if you haven't got kids, you're probably too busy having a life. The letters are very much associated with the nuclear family. It's like you have to have the ideal life before you can put pen to paper.'

The point is, though, that no-one puts pen to paper to write a round-robin. In the past round-robins were always typewritten – for expediency, but also to give an aura of 'published' importance. The look of them always reminds me obscurely of my friend Huw, who, after acquiring a laminating machine for some sixth-form art project, went through a phase of laminating till receipts, shopping lists, etc 'to make them look special'. Nowadays round-robins are bashed out on the family laptop while Cosmo and Jocasta watch an improving 70s-vintage children's TV drama and sip home-made elderflower cordial.

Round-robins are impersonal machine-writing notable for their authors' inability to tell the wood from the trees: seismic events like the death of a parent warrant the same amount of space as a ferry journey to a Greek island. There is either too much detail or too little. And as for materiality… you're supposed to jump for joy when that folded-up A4 insert tumbles out of the card. But it might as well be a flyer for a new takeaway. You're lucky if anyone has bothered to sign it or append a biro-scrawled 'personal bit' (usually something like 'Hope we see you in the new year!!! Let's really make an effort!!!!!!'). Actually, no you're not.

The very idea of writing a letter to *more than one person at once* is ludicrous. Letters should be precision-targeted. Moreover, if you have experienced something and consider that an account of that experience might benefit a person, you should sharpen your powers of observation on the whetstone of a letter like Samuel Johnson's superb 'From a country gentleman in town, to his brother in the country, describing a public execution in London', one of his Familiar Letters:

> *I have this day been satisfying a curiosity, I believe natural to most people, by seeing an execution at*

Tyburn... All the way up Holborn the croud was so great, as, at every twenty or thirty yards, to obstruct the passage; and wine, notwithstanding a late good order against that practice, was brought the malefactors, who drank greedily of it, which I thought did not suit well with their deplorable circumstances... [The men] swore, laugh'd, and talked obscenely; and wished their wicked companions good luck, with as much assurance as if their employment had been the most lawful.

And as soon as the poor creatures were half-dead, I was much surprised, before such a number of peace-officers, to see the populace fall to hauling and pulling the carcases with so much earnestness, as to occasion several warm encounters, and broken heads... [Among these were] persons sent by private surgeons to obtain bodies for dissection. The contests between these were fierce and bloody, and frightful to look at.

This is bracing, novelistic stuff. But its power derives from its specificity of focus, just as Lady Mary Wortley Montagu's account of the hot baths at Sophia does. For Lady Mary brings saucy news from an alien planet:

I believe, upon the whole, there were two hundred

women, and yet none of those disdainful smiles, and satirical whispers, that never fail in our assemblies, when any body appears that is not dressed exactly in the fashion. They repeated over and over to me; 'U*ʒ*elle, pek u*ʒ*elle', which is nothing but, Charming, very charming. —— The first sofas were covered with cushions and rich carpets, on which sat the ladies; and on the second, their slaves behind them, but without any distinction of rank by their dress, all being in the state of nature, that is, in plain English, stark naked, without any beauty or defect concealed. Yet there was not the least wanton smile or immodest gesture amongst them. They walked and moved with the same majestic grace, which Milton describes our general mother with. There were many amongst them, as exactly proportioned as ever any goddess was drawn by the pencil of a Guido or Titian, — and most of their skins shiningly white, only adorned by their beautiful hair divided into many tresses, hanging on their shoulders, braided either with pearl or ribbon, perfectly representing the figures of the Graces.

I was here convinced of the truth of a reflection I have often made, that if it were the fashion to go naked, the face would be hardly observed. I perceived, that the ladies of the most delicate skins and finest shapes had the greatest share of *my admiration, though their faces were sometimes less beautiful than those of their companions. To tell you the truth, I had wickedness enough, to wish secretly, that Mr Gervais could have been there invisible. I fancy it would have very much improved his art, to see so many fine women naked, in different postures, some in conversation, some working, others drinking coffee or sherbet, and many negligently lying on their cushions, while their slaves (generally pretty girls of seventeen or eighteen) were employed in braiding their hair in several pretty fancies. In short, 'tis the women's coffee-house, where all the news of the town is told, scandal invented, &c. ———— They generally take this diversion once a-week, and stay there at least four or five hours, without getting cold by immediate coming out of the hot bath into the cold room, which was very surprising to me. The lady, that seemed the most considerable among them, entreated me to sit by her, and would fain have undressed me for the bath. I excused myself with some difficulty. They being however all so earnest in persuading me, I was at last forced to open my shirt, and shew them my stays; which satisfied them very well; for, I saw, they believed I was locked up in that machine, and that it was not in my own power to open it, which contrivance they attributed to my husband,*

———— *I was charmed with their civility and beauty, and should have been very glad to pass more time with them; but Mr W———— resolving to pursue his journey next morning early, I was in haste to see the ruins of Justinian's church, which did not afford me so agreeable a prospect as I had left, being little more than a heap of stones.*

Adieu, madam, I am sure I have now entertained you with an account of such a sight as you never saw in your life, and what no book of travels could inform you of, as 'tis no less than death for a man to be found in one of these places.

The Joy of Nothing

Of course, letters don't *have* to be full of news. As long as it's done well, the Letter With Nothing Much To Say Except 'Hi' can be just as rich and rewarding.

The king of phatic letters is our old friend William Cowper. He resorted to the phatic partly as a point of principle, but also because his life was so dominated by religious devotion that there wasn't much else to it.

While living in Huntingdon with his friends the Unwins, he spent the morning '[reading] either the scripture, or the sermons of some faithful preacher of those holy mysteries'. Church was at 11am, after which he was at liberty to read, walk, ride or work in the garden until dinner at 3pm. In the garden afterwards 'I have generally the pleasure of religious conversation till tea-time'. After tea, typically, came a four-mile walk, then 'at night we read and converse, as before, till supper, and commonly finish the evening either with hymns or a sermon; and last of all the family are called to prayers'.

If you read that last paragraph without feeling a strong urge to play naked Twister then give yourself an extra doughnut.

This letter, written to William Unwin on August 6, 1780 when Cowper was 49, is wryly wise about the importance of process in any kind of correspondence – in making an effort for the sake of making an effort because, in undertaking to correspond, you have established a form of social contract.

> *You like to hear from me – this is a very good reason why I should write – but I have nothing to say – this seems equally a good reason why I should not. Yet if you had alighted from your horse at our door this morning, and at this present writing, being 5 o'clock in the afternoon, had found occasion to say to me, Mr Cowper, you have not spoke since I came in, have you resolved never to speak again? it would be but a poor reply if in answer to the summons I should plead inability as my best & only excuse. And this by the way, suggests to me a seasonable piece of instruction, and reminds me of what I am very apt to forget when I have my epistolary business in hand: that a letter may be written upon any thing or nothing, just as that any thing or nothing happens to occur...*

A letter is written, as a conversation is maintained, or a journey perform'd, not by preconcerted or premeditated means, by a new contrivance, or an invention never heard of before, but merely by maintaining a progress, and resolving as a postillion does, having once set out, never to stop till we reach the appointed end. If a man may talk without thinking, why may he not write upon the same terms?

It's a good question. But of course the answer is: because not every man can write as fluently and funnily as Cowper.

Jane Austen and her sister Cassandra wrote to each other frequently. The letters are full of balls. Balls, and suitors, and praise for each other's efforts. (Jane: 'I am very much flattered by your commendation of my last Letter, for I write only for Fame, and without any view to pecuniary Emolument.') Only 160 letters from Jane have survived. The earliest known one was written when she was twenty – no longer a child, plainly; yet the relationship the letters trace is that of two children who grew up together.

As I mentioned earlier, the value of Austen's letters has been disputed over the years. They give a reliable picture of late-eighteenth-century upper-middle-class life, but are not profound. RW Chapman calls them 'unstudied': 'Their themes are accidental; their bulk, that of a quarto sheet.' They aren't coherent, he complains; they are fragmentary, and lack plot.

Jane's most recent biographer, Claire Tomalin, locates the source of the letters' sometimes dislikeable tone in her subject's childhood, specifically the emotional distance between Jane and her mother, who farmed Jane and her six siblings out to wet nurses until they were old enough to be 'socially acceptable':

> *The most striking aspect of Jane's adult letters is their defensiveness. They lack tenderness towards herself as much as towards others. You are aware of the inner creature, deeply responsive and alive, but mostly you are faced with the hard shell; and sometimes a claw is put out, and a sharp nip is given to whatever offends. They are the letters of someone who does not open her heart; and in the adult who avoids intimacy you sense the child who was uncertain where to expect love or to look for security, and armoured herself against rejection.*

When Jane and Cassandra were apart they wrote to each other every three or four days, beginning another letter as soon as the previous one had been posted. There is a formula to them, as their editor Deirdre Le Faye explains: 'There is always a first letter from Jane telling Cassandra of the journey from home to the destination; then a series of letters talking about daily events at the other place; and one or more letters planning the journey home...'

Sometimes there is nothing to write about except the lack of things to write about:

> I am not surprised, my dear Cassandra, that you did not find my last Letter very full of Matter, & I wish this may not have the same deficiency; — but we are doing nothing ourselves to write about, & I am therefore quite dependant upon the Communications of our friends, or my own Wit.

And So to War

Britain's postal system began life, as we have seen, as a courier service between monarch and army. At first it was a portal for military intelligence: personal messages were the exception not the rule; and anyway, most common soldiers were illiterate.

But this changed. Many soldiers learned to read and write for the specific purpose of writing letters home. Reduced postal rates were granted to the army and navy in 1795, and four years later an army postmaster was appointed to accompany the army overseas and ensure mail was distributed to troops. Why? Because letters were vital to morale, as this 1809 letter from a British officer based in Portugal demonstrates:

> *I received your letter of the 12th two days ago. You cannot tell how pleased I was to receive a letter in so short a time. It lessens the distance between us so much especially when I recollect I was frequently*

longer in Ireland without a letter. As we have few books and not much evening society, you can have no idea of the joy a letter from home brings – on the contrary if a mail does arrive without a letter it is quite a disappointment.

Letters became relics of the battlefield and often arrived in a packet alongside bloody locks of hair. Sometimes enemy soldiers scavenged them and sent them home as souvenirs. Sometimes letters found on or near a soldier's body after death were the quickest means of identifying him: a story in a Gettysburg paper, the *Adams Sentinel,* on July 28, 1863, told how

> *One day last week, among the relics of the dreadful fight, there was picked up by a soldier... a small paper, which contained two separate locks of hair attached thereto, directed to Mr Wellerford, from Louisiana, by his wife, in a beautiful handwriting. Below one lock was Fanny Wellerford, below the other Richard Wellerford – and below both 'Our darlings!'*

For many families, letters were the only way to stay in touch with fathers, sons and brothers who had been posted abroad. Jane Austen wrote regularly to her brother Frank, a captain in the navy, keeping him up to date with gossip. In one letter she asks his permission to mention the name of his ship, HMS *Elephant*, in the novel she is writing (*Mansfield Park*):

> *You will be glad to hear that every Copy of S&S is sold & that it has brought me £140 — besides the Copyright, if that should ever be of any value. — I have now therefore written myself into £250. — which only makes me long for more. — I have something in hand — which I hope on the credit of P&P will sell well, tho' not half so entertaining. And by the bye — shall you object to my mentioning the Elephant in it, & two or three other of your old Ships? — I have done it, but it shall not stay, to make you angry. — They are only just mentioned.*

Austen's jaunty, chatty tone is just right, just what you imagine Frank would have wanted to hear. But then they are siblings, communicating in sibling shorthand. You would expect more angst in letters from wives to husbands, something more along the lines of Samuel Richardson's suggested formula in 'A Wife to her Husband at Sea' from his *Familiar Letters*... :

I think it a long time since I have had the comfort and satisfaction of hearing of your welfare. Often and often do I reflect on the unhappiness of us poor women, who are marry'd to seafaring men. Every wind that blows, every pirate we hear of, and now, in time of war, every hour of our lives, the dread of enemies alarms us. God's providence is our reliance, and so it ought, for nothing else can sustain us...

A popular Victorian genre was the soldier's 'life-and-letters' celebrating Empire and noble sacrifice. *Twelve Years of a Soldier's Life in India* (1859) collects extracts from the letters of the late Major WSR Hodson – vignettes of expat life interspersed with campaign minutiae and public-school philosophising:

We are under much stricter discipline in this corps, both officers and men, and obliged to be orderly and submissive. No bad thing for us either. I hold there is more real liberty in being under a decent restraint than in absolute freedom from any check.

Though they are sometimes formulaic, and may have been written 'into' a readership that expected reassuring tales of derring-do, these letters are more honest (and their authors frequently more

open-minded and inquisitive) than we're inclined
to give them credit for.

Twelve Years... is edited and introduced by Major
Hodson's brother, Reverend George Hodson, who
explains:

> *[The] letters, written in all the freedom of unre-*
> *served intercourse, will give a truer notion of his*
> *character than the most laboured description; they*
> *exhibit the undercurrent of deep feelings that ran*
> *through even his most playful moods, the yearning*
> *after home that mingled with the dreams of ambi-*
> *tion and the thirst for the excitement of war, the*
> *almost womanly tenderness that co-existed with*
> *the stern determination of the soldier.*

The years in which his brother was away in India
were 'those years in which his character received
its mature development'. During this time, the
Reverend admits, he knew Hodson 'only by his
letters':

> *My recollections of him, vivid as they are, are not*
> *of the leader of men in council and the battle-field,*
> *but of the bright and joyous boy, the life of the home*

*circle, the tender and affectionate son, the loving
brother, the valued friend, the popular companion.*

This is one of the points where we glimpse the
sadness lurking beneath the determination to cast
his brother's life as a medieval romance. The letters
stand in for the absent soldier, become in some
respects more real than the absent soldier, and
when the soldier is killed he is valorised as the sum
of his epistolary output no matter how boring and
incontinent it is.

This might be because there is no body to send
home.

The American Civil War was notable for the
quantity of soldiers' corpses left in hospitals or on
the battlefield then buried in mass graves because
they were too disfigured or decomposed to return
to grieving families. In this situation, letters were
all those families had to work with.

But some soldiers had straightforwardly
careerist ambitions. Aware that they were experi-
encing something historically momentous, they
wrote with an eye on future publication. Erskine
Childers, future author of the espionage classic *The
Riddle of the Sands*, fought briefly in the Boer War
before being invalided out for trench foot. While
in South Africa he wrote regularly to his sisters,

requesting that the letters be kept safe for his return. The sisters showed them to a friend who showed them to a publisher and lo – they formed the basis of his first book, *In the Ranks of the CIV.*

The cheeriness of some soldiers' letters can be hard to credit. And the further down the chain of social class you go, the more sense you get of letters being written to maintain a civilian identity rather than uphold a patriotic ideal. I love this one from Private Harry Cooper to his friend Mr Pickles, sent from Spearman's Kopje during the Boer War. Paper being scarce, it was written on cigarette papers, a piece of brown cartridge paper and a luggage label:

I have had excellent health up to this, but I am getting very thin – you can tell how thin I am when I say that I put my straps on the other day and they fell off me. I am sure I can get down a rifle barrel easy enough. I haven't had a shave for two months. Both my trousers knees are worn out, and another important part of my unmentionables is gone also. To tell the truth, I could get a better rig-out at a rag-shop. Roll on Ladysmith! We attack again tomorrow. We will get in this time. It was my birthday yesterday – that makes one in Aldershot, another in Ireland and the last in South Africa, so that is not bad for three years' service. I met Harry Mount (Private Mount, of Beachcliffe – 1st Durham Light Infantry) on the 3rd. He was on sentry on the pontoon bridge… I can tell you it is as good as a circus to see us sometimes. We can't get a wash for three days. But never mind, I don't care a jot so long as I don't get shot. I shall be very, very glad when we get to Pretoria. I shall have to close now as I have only another 'tag' paper left. Give my best respects to all enquiring friend. Au revoir!

Actual physical letters remain important to servicemen and -women, especially when they're stationed abroad, and despite the prevalence of texts, email, Skype, etc. Organisations like My Soldier and Soldiers' Angels exist to encourage and facilitate the sending of these letters to US forces. 'When you adopt you are committing to sending a card or letter each week,' advises the Soldiers' Angels website, 'and a *minimum* of one or two care packages a month.' (A stern note at the bottom of the page reminds potential adopters: 'This is a serious job for serious people. This is *not* a dating service, and we do not tolerate improper or inappropriate behaviour.')

Military historian Siân Price spent three years reading over 30,000 soldiers' letters while researching her recent book *If You're Reading This…: Last Letters from the Front Line*. 'There is something very beautiful about reading the intimate thoughts of these men who knew they could be about to die,' Price said. 'The common theme that binds them all is love.'

She's right, of course. But now that the tradition of the reportage-based 'testimonial' soldier's letter has passed, what's left can resemble a suicide note in its bare brevity. Here is Gunner Lee Thornton writing to his fiancée Helen before he was killed in Iraq aged 22: 'I don't know why I am writing this because I really hope that this never gets to you, because if it does that means I am dead.'

I really hope that this never gets to you. Imagine having to write such a letter – a letter which, among other things, forces you to conceptualise death when *not* conceptualising death is a necessary part of your job.

War poet Wilfred Owen's letters were censored before publication by his brother Harold, who went to work with scissors and Indian ink – ironic when you consider that this was one of Wilfred's jobs on the Western Front. 'Today's letters were rather interesting,' he writes to his mother on January 10, 1917. 'The Daddys' letters are specially touching, and the number of xxx to sisters and mothers weigh more in heaven than Victoria Crosses.' A few months later, however, he will be numbed and affectless, brutalised by what he has witnessed: 'I [now] don't take the cigarette out of my mouth when I write Deceased over their letters.'

Owen was alert to what it was and wasn't possible to say or include in letters home: 'I am not allowed to send a sketch, but you must know I am transformed now, wearing a steel helmet, buff jerkin of leather, rubber-waders up to the hips, & gauntlets.' He found letter-writing 'a fitter mode of intimate communication than speaking' and told his mother to keep his letters in lieu of the diary he was not writing. The letters are intense, and keenly descriptive – both on the surface and beneath it: Owen had agreed a code with his mother, the 'mistletoe code', where after the appearance of that word she was to take the second letter of each line and spell out the place where he was stationed.

Sometimes meaning and syntax buckled under the strain. In one letter deploying the code Owen has written 'not so bad' in the margin to signal approval of his own subtlety.

Nowadays an email would be forwarded to any interested parties. Given the graphic nature of his letters' content, however, Owen is firm about whom he wants to see them: 'Don't pass round these sheets but have portions typed for Leslie etc.'

Requests for cigarettes and tins of boracic rub up against nightmarish reportage, all the more harrowing for Owen's awareness, flatly stated, that this mechanised slaughter is occurring as his mother takes tea or goes to church. But then she is a world apart: 'It seems wrong that even your dear handwriting should come into such a Gehenna as this.'

His most famous letter, produced after a week spent holding a dugout near Beaumont Hamel ('cobbled with skulls'), reads like a poem:

I can see no excuse for deceiving you about these last four days.
I have suffered seventh hell.
I have not been at the front.
I have been in front of it.

And of course, there are the enclosures... 'Here is a gas poem, done yesterday,' he writes, referring to 'Dulce et Decorum Est'.

Owen manages to sound jaunty even about his shellshock, for which he will be invalided to Craiglockhart War Hospital, the site of his meeting with fellow poet Siegfried Sassoon.

You know it was not the Bosche that worked me up, nor the explosives, but it was living so long

*by poor old Cock Robin (as we used to call 2/
Lt Gaukroger), who lay not only near by, but in
various places around and about, if you understand. I hope you don't!*

His final letter home was written at 6.15pm on
October 31, 1918:

*So thick is the smoke in this cellar that I can hardly
see by a candle 12 ins. away, and so thick are the
inmates that I can hardly write for pokes, nudges &
jolts… There is no danger down here, or if any, it
will be well over before you read these lines.*

He died four days later, a week before the war
ended.

(A soldier's death was often signalled by a lapse
in correspondence long before any official telegram
arrived. Thus any unanticipated silence was a cause
for extreme alarm. Imagine…)

War accelerates maturity, forcing people to change
and adapt beyond all expectations. War can be
a stunting, retarding event to live through in the

sense that it 'steals' chunks of a person's life; but also revelatory.

Letters written in wartime can't give you the big picture – just a tiny glimpse, and one that may seem irrelevant, may be nothing more than the novelist and dandy Julian Maclaren-Ross at the end of 1939 trying to persuade the BBC to accept his plays for broadcasting. (Maclaren-Ross, incidentally, wrote many of his letters on the complimentary stationery provided by the expensive London hotels where he liked to blow his meagre earnings. His biographer Paul Willetts observes that 'down the lefthand margins there are usually small sepia photos of that establishment's facilities: ornate Turkish baths, winter gardens, ballrooms…')

War enabled many young soldiers to come of age in exotic, alien surroundings. It was a charged business for them, but equally so for those left behind.

Novelist Iris Murdoch and fellow Oxford student and Communist Party member Frank Thompson began to correspond in earnest in March 1941 after Thompson was transferred from the Royal Artillery to 'Phantom', a small intelligence unit based in the Middle East. The letters, many of them wartime 'airgraphs' – quarto sheets transferred to microfilm, then developed and magnified at their destination – show war's maturing effects nicely. For the young

Murdoch is rather a poser. She knows this, to be fair, and admits to being 'full of pretences & attitudes'. Her early letters treat the world as a grand abstraction, books the only concrete reality. But the tone changes as the war progresses: 'Oh Frank, I wonder & I wonder what the future holds for us all – shall we ever make out of the dreamy idealistic stuff of our lives any hard & real thing? You will perhaps.'

Over the course of the correspondence Murdoch falls in love with Thompson. But he is killed on an SOE mission in Serbia in November 1943. In his last letter he tells her: 'I can honestly say I've never been in love. When I pined for you I was too young to know what I was doing – no offence meant.'

A friend of mine has a fascinating cache of letters that her father, Alfred, wrote to his sister Alice during WW2 when he was in the Royal Army Medical Corp. The early letters, written while he was still training in Abergavenny with the 45th Infantry Field Hygiene Section, are jaunty, joking, concerned to entertain as well as inform ('We had a special Xmas dinner but to make up for it they gave us no tea or supper').

In a letter dated March 3, 1940, he announces that he and his girlfriend, Catherine, are getting engaged. But by the end of the year clouds have appeared. He has found the courage to break off the engagement, which he had felt uneasy about and pressured into. Curiously, this most important letter, dated December 23, 1940, is written to his mother and father in pencil (because he needed to keep amending it as he was writing?) and on paper torn from a book. The handwriting is subtly different, too. My friend has a theory that it's actually a fair copy of the letter made by his sister, perhaps because the original was torn up or thrown away in a rage by his parents, who wanted the engagement to go ahead.

'You are no doubt thinking I am a bit of a cad by doing all this at Christmas time,' Alfred begins, but what follows is an explanation, not an apology:

When I came into the Army against my will, over 12 months ago, I was young with little experience of the outside world. I had just passed my examination only to see my hopes of a really good job & career shattered by war. Twelve months of army routine travelling all over England & latterly being shouldered with terrific responsibilities in my work have changed my whole outlook on life. I have grown older & shaken off the boyish ways such as I had when I first knew Catherine. In consideration of my experience these last 12 months & of my age, I submit that I am well qualified to take decisions which affect my whole life.

The decision to ask Catherine to relieve me of my responsibilities towards her was reached after very careful & deliberate thought for a variety of reasons. Chief reason, was I could see endless little quarrels followed by threats. Nothing is further from my head than to upset my own Father & Mother to whom I owe so much, but now I must tell you this. On two occasions to my face & on one occasion in a letter Catherine has threatened to take her life. Each time it was not due to anything I had done. In all fairness I beg you to consider this & just how I feel about it when I realise that I should probably have to go through life with the constant fear of these threats.

Wilfred Owen's most famous poem takes its title from an ode by the Roman poet Horace: *Dulce et decorum est pro patria mori* – 'How sweet and fitting it is to die for one's country'. The next line is less well known: *mors et fugacem persequitur virum* – 'Death pursues the man who flees'.

What makes Alfred's letter so moving is its self-aware determination not to flee from a difficult situation. You sense him trying out a formal, adult tone he had probably never used before, least of all with his parents. It must be a third or fourth draft: its composition betrays all the 'very careful & deliberate thought' that precipitated the split.

The war has, he says, 'shattered' his life and hopes for the future. But in his heart he knows this isn't quite true: the war has given him purpose and direction. Besides, in peacetime the relationship with Catherine might have drifted on without ever being forced to a crisis.

Alfred, who died in 2000, never spoke about the incident afterwards. This uncharacteristic, materially dubious letter is the only proof that it occurred.

Straight to the Heart

Love letters are letters-to-the-power-of-a-hundred. All the arguments rehearsed earlier in this book about the value of slow communication and materiality hold particularly for love letters, which are cherished and preserved above all others. But while the love letter can be one of the most heartfelt, authentic modes, it can also fall to earth faster than a flame-haired pop star with wonky eyes.

Nothing is as fatuous and overblown as a fatuous, overblown love letter. To make matters worse, love letters are often (though by no means always) expressions of happiness; and as the playwright Montherlant observed: 'Happiness writes in white ink on a white page.' It isn't memorable or interesting.

Read a load of love letters in one sitting and the effect is close to nauseating: too much confectionery, too rich. Other people's love can make us feel inferior. And reading your *own* love letters, especially ten or more years after the event, is a bone-tingling sensation.

Old love letters conjure spectres from tombs. Their totemic quality can be negative, like a curse, and the idea that we hang on to letters from lovers because if we destroyed them we'd be destroying ourselves is explored in a Thomas Hardy poem called, appropriately, 'The Love-Letters':

> *I met him quite by accident*
> *In a bye-path that he'd frequent.*
> *And, as he neared, the sunset glow*
> *Warmed up the smile of pleasantry*
> *Upon his too thin face, while he*
> *Held a square packet up to me,*
> *Of what, I did not know.*
>
> *Well, said he then; they are my old letters*
> *Perhaps she – rather felt them fetters...*
> *You see, I am in a slow decline,*
> *And she's broken off with me.*
>
> *Quite right*
> *To send them back, and true foresight;*
> *I'd got too fond of her!*
> *To-night I burn them – stuff of mine!*

He laughed in the sun – an ache in his laughter –
And went. I heard of his death soon after.

(No letters exist between Hardy and his first wife Emma apart from two fragments copied by Hardy into his notebooks: Emma burned them all in the garden.)

The love letters most commonly cited in early exemplary manuals are Ovid's *Heroides*, Pliny the Younger's letters to his wife Calpurnia and the medieval letters of Heloise and Abelard.

The *Heroides* are letter-poems from early in Ovid's writing career, ostensibly the work of the great heroines of myth and legend. So we have Hero writing not very feministly to Leander: 'I cannot be patient for Love! We burn with equal fires, but I am not equal to you in strength; men methinks must have stronger natures. As the body, so is the soul of women frail. Delay but a little longer and I shall die!'

Penelope, on the other hand, is less supine and frankly impatient with the whole letter-as-proxy-for-person thing: 'This your Penelope sends to you, too-slow Ulysses; a letter in return does me no good; come yourself!'

Top Roman lawyer Pliny was 39 when he married for the third time in AD 100. Calpurnia, his bride, was fourteen. Their marriage was unusual not for this reason – fourteen wasn't considered all that young – but because they actually loved each other.

> *You say that you are feeling my absence very much,' he writes to her, 'and your only comfort when I am not there is to hold my writings in your hand and often put them in my place by your side... I too am always reading your letters, and returning to them again and again as if they were new to me – but this only fans the fire of my longing for you. If your letters are so dear to me, you can imagine how I delight in your company. Do write as often as you can, although you give me pleasure mingled with pain.*

Peter Abelard was a highly regarded French philosopher in the early twelfth century. Heloise, his beautiful student, was the niece of one Canon Fulbert. When Abelard decided, in his thirties, that he wanted to experience those pleasures he had hitherto denied himself, etc, etc, he made Heloise his quarry.

Now, Heloise lived with her uncle. So Abelard went to the Canon and, claiming he could not afford a house of his own, asked to lodge with his family. He would pay some of the rent and make up the rest by giving Heloise, um, 'special tutorials'.

Surprise! – Heloise and Abelard became lovers despite the 22-year age gap between them. Long after rumours of the affair had swept Paris, the Canon found out. (See picture below: that's him, bursting into the room, finding out.)

He sent his kinsmen to Abelard's house, where they castrated him. Heloise, who was pregnant with their child Astrolabe, entered a convent. Abelard was exiled to Brittany and became a monk. The lovers never met again but sent each other passionate letters remembering the intensity of their lost love and struggling to reconcile it with their new duty to stay chaste. (Thought: presumably it was fairly easy for Abelard to stay chaste, seeing as he had no genitals?)

You couldn't ask for a better justification of the practice of writing love letters than this, from one of Heloise's efforts:

If a picture, which is but a mute representation of an object, can give such pleasure, what cannot letters inspire? They have souls; they can speak; they have in them all that force which expresses the transports of the heart; they have all the fire of our passions, they can raise them as much as if the persons themselves were present; they have all the tenderness and the delicacy of speech, and sometimes even a boldness of expression beyond it.

We may write to each other; so innocent a pleasure is not denied us. Let us not lose through negligence the only happiness which is left us, and the only one perhaps which the malice of our enemies can never ravish from us. I shall read that you are my husband and you shall see me sign myself your wife. In spite of all our misfortunes you may be what you please in your letter. Letters were first invented for consoling such solitary wretches as myself. Having lost the substantial pleasures of seeing and possessing you, I shall in some measure compensate this loss by the satisfaction I shall find in your writing. There I shall read your most sacred thoughts; I shall carry them always about with me, I shall kiss them every moment; if you can be capable of any jealousy let it be for the fond caresses I shall bestow upon your letters, and envy only the happiness of those rivals. That writing may be no trouble to you, write always to me carelessly and without study; I had rather read the dictates of the heart than of the brain. I cannot live if you will not tell me that you still love me; but that language ought to be so natural to you, that I believe you cannot speak otherwise to me without violence to yourself.

A letter like this has tremendous rhetorical power. But is it suitable and useful as a model? It's hard to be prescriptive when it comes to love letters, isn't it? Because surely anything goes? To legislate is in some way to violate intimacy.

That said, we violate intimacy every time we read a love letter that wasn't written by or sent to us. 'The frankest and freest product of the human mind and heart is a love letter,' wrote Mark Twain in the introduction to his autobiography. 'The writer gets his limitless freedom of statement and expression from his sense that no stranger is going to see what he is writing.'

Well – up to a point, Lord Copper.

George Saintsbury, writing not long after the publication of Keats's letters to his fiancée Fanny

Brawne in 1878 – an event he deplores – urges his readers not to give in to the base impulse to snoop: 'There are, it is to be hoped, few people who read such letters (unless they are of such a date that Time has exercised his strange power of resanctifying desecration and making private property public) without an unpleasant consciousness of eavesdropping.'

It's amazing, though, the number of ways we have of persuading ourselves that reading other people's mail is morally legit. Remember Leo in LP Hartley's *The Go-Between*? He agrees to carry letters between Marian, his posh friend's sister, and Ted Burgess, the farmer she is 'spooning'. When, one day, Marian accidentally gives Leo an unsealed letter to take to Ted, he wonders disingenuously if 'she hadn't left it open on purpose, so that I could find out something which would be useful to both of us'.

No no no no NO!!! DON'T DO IT, LEO!

But of course he does – well, he peeks into the envelope at 'the words that were exposed' (arf), and finds not even a love letter but a sex letter, an inarticulate shriek of desire:

Darling, darling, darling,
Same place, same time, this evening.
But take care not to –

(It's tame stuff, admittedly, compared to James Joyce's porny letters to his wife and muse Nora Barnacle calling her, among other things, his 'darling brown-arsed fuckbird' – but even so.)

If we can't read the letters themselves, we can enjoy the vicarious thrill of watching their recipients read. Of Vermeer's six epistolary scenes, the most intriguing is 'Young Girl Reading a Letter by an Open Window' (c1657).

A young Dutch woman stands reading a letter. Red drapery hangs over the top of the glass – it looks as if it has blown inwards, exposing the woman to the street below. The letter is crimped at the edges where her hands have held it: clearly, she has read it intently. In the foreground is a table laden with fruit. A peach has been sliced open to reveal its stone.

The letter the girl is reading is, plainly, a love letter. That would be obvious without the additional knowledge that Vermeer originally painted a putto of Cupid on the wall behind her which X-rays have detected beneath the mass of green drapery.

If the woman looked up, at her reflection in the window-pane, she might see us looking at her, invading her privacy.

Sometimes, though, our ignoble desire to read private letters is matched by a letter-writer's ignoble desire to be read. No-one understood the PR value of letters – even 'private' ones to lovers – better than George Gordon, aka Lord Byron.

Published in 1830, only six years after its subject's death, Thomas Moore's *Letters and Journals of Lord Byron* had been on the boil since 1818, when Byron abandoned plans to write his autobiography. It was

a collaborative effort. Byron allowed Moore to use his letters and knew full well the impact their publication would have (though he also knew that Moore would censor the worst bits).

The boastful, I-am-a-sex-god letters Byron wrote to friends like the clergyman(!) and social reformer John Thomas Becher are almost ludicrous:

Dorant's Hotel, Feb 26, 1808

My dear Becher, — Just rising from my Bed, having been up till six at a Masquerade, I find your letter... I am worse than ever, to give you some idea of my late life, I have this moment received a prescription from Pearson, not for any complaint but from debility, and literally too much love... In fact, my blue-eyed Caroline, who is only sixteen, has been lately so charming, that though we are both in perfect health, we are at present commanded to repose, being nearly worn out...

In another letter, written later that evening, he records how 'we supped with seven whores, a Bawd and a Ballet-master in Madame Catalan's apartment' where he considered 'purchasing' a few of the students.

He continues: 'I am buried in an abyss of

Sensuality, I have renounced hazard however, but I am given to Harlots, and live in a state of Concubinage.'

And so on.

Byron's most intriguing relationship was with Lady Caroline Lamb (not the blue-eyed Caroline mentioned above). Skinny and androgynous – she liked to dress as a page-boy – 'Caro' pursued Byron obsessively after reading his poem 'Childe Harold's Pilgrimage' and bequeathed us the cliché that he was 'mad, bad, and dangerous to know'.

Over the course of their five-month affair, which started in May 1812 and scandalised London, they sent each other over 300 letters of which sadly few have survived.

Caroline's first letter to Byron told him that he deserved to be happy and should not 'throw away such Talents as you possess in gloom & regrets for the past'. Her second, written 48 hours later, was a parody of the opening of 'Childe Harold'. This set the pattern: it was not unusual, thereafter, for them to write to each other several times a day.

Caroline was already married to William Lamb, but their marriage was in trouble. One of their children had died, another was autistic, and William had eccentric sexual needs that she disliked meeting.

In the end Byron reciprocated and the pair were

briefly inseparable, despite uncertainty on Byron's part as to whether he actually fancied Caroline. Soon, however, Byron grew bored. Caroline's reaction was to bombard him with love letters, which he ignored. One day she turned up at Byron's house in disguise. When asked to leave she refused, instead grabbing a knife and trying to stab herself. She didn't succeed; Byron restrained her until she had calmed down.

On August 9, 1812, she took materiality to an extreme by sending Byron clippings of her pubic hair and a letter which read:

> *I asked you not to send blood but Yet do — because if it means love I like to have it. I cut the hair too close & bled much more than you need — do not you the same & pray put not scissors points near where quei capelli grow — sooner take it from the arm or wrist — pray be careful…*

Having alienated her family, Caroline fled to Ireland at Byron's suggestion. While she was there he sent her a letter whose regular inclusion in anthologies belies its casual, signing-off-now-thanks cruelty. By the time Caroline received it, its author had already moved on to his next lover, the much older Jane Elizabeth, countess of Oxford.

My dearest Caroline,

If the tears, which you saw, and I know I am not apt to shed; if the agitation in which I parted from you – agitation which you must have perceived through the whole of this nervous affair, did not commence till the moment of leaving you approached; if all I have said and done, and am still but too ready to say and do, have not sufficiently proved what my feelings are, and must ever be, towards you, my love, I have no other proof to offer...

'Promise not to love you'? Ah, Caroline, it is past promising! But I shall attribute all concessions to the proper motive, and never cease to feel all that you have already witnessed, and more than ever can be known, but to my own heart – perhaps, to yours. May God forgive, protect and bless you ever and ever, more than ever – Your most attached

Byron

Where Is the Top and How Do You Go over It?

Love, we are told, is a many-splendoured thing, and as such deserving of any rhetorical hoop you care to throw at it.

Or is it? Aren't the most effective love letters actually restrained, uncertain, egoless?

Think of Flaubert writing to George Sand: 'I don't know what sort of feeling I have for you, but I have a particular tenderness for you, and one I have never felt for anyone, up to now. We understood each other, didn't we, that was good.'

Or Dylan Thomas to his wife Caitlin in late 1936: 'I want this to be a letter full of news, but there isn't any yet. It's just a letter full of what I think about you and me. You're not empty, empty still now, are you? Have you got love to send me?'

Or Clementine Churchill, in November 1909, reassuring a stressed Winston with a familiar litany of cutesy nicknames:

My Beloved Darling One

*Your letter has just come & I am writing you a line
to tell you how much I think of my Pug all day &
of all the struggles, difficulties & complications he
is encountering just now, more than ever...*

*The PK [aka their daughter Diana] sends you
a heavenly smile – She is lying in her little cot &
her darling little face looks like a creamy rosebud
crowned with gold –*

Goodbye & Good Cheer my Sweet heart
Your own
Clemmie Kat

Love letters between married couples have a
particular flavour. Our reading of them is influ-
enced by what we know about the marriage. The
Churchills' was broadly happy and we read the
letters accordingly. But, for example, the marriage
of Jane and Thomas Carlyle was one of the most
unhappy and dysfunctional in Victorian literary
London.

So a letter that might strike a reader ignorant of
this as merely over-solicitous seems to the reader
who knows better *enragingly* windy, fussy and
controlling, never mind the profusion of endearments ('Dearest Wifekin', 'My little Heartkin', etc).

Here is Thomas to Jane on May 21, 1834. He is down in London house-hunting and has, in fact, just found the house at Cheyne Walk where they will spend the rest of their married lives. Jane is still in Scotland but will shortly be joining him in London:

As to thy own voyage, poor Goody, I have only to advise that thou take some finest ham sandwiches, or other the like ware, with a thimbleful of good brandy; and depend as little on the dirty little Highland Steward, or Cumberland Stewardess (a good body nevertheless) as may be; also that thou take abundance of wrappages, and sit as much on deck as possible (there sickness can be in general escaped); and finally commend thyself with hopeful Patience to God's guidance, and think that every bound of the boat is bringing thee nearer to me, to thy home my heart.

Lucky old Jane! The boat is bringing nearer to her a crotchety, impotent proto-fascist!

Eight years earlier, on June 28, 1826, Jane had stated her make-do-and-mend philosophy of marriage in one of the weirdest love letters ever written:

Dearest —

I know not what in all the world to say to you. I cannot write nowadays; I cannot think; my head and heart are in an endless whirl, which no words can express. In short, this marriage, I find, is like death: so long as it is uncertain in its approach, one can expect it with a surprising indifference; but certain, looked in the face within a definite term, it becomes a matter of most tremendous interest. — Yet think not that I wish it but as it is — No! 'ce que je fait je le ferois encore' [What I have done I would do again]: for if I am not without fear, my hope is far greater than my fear.

Oh yes — the whole arrangement will do excellently well: at least it will be our own faults if it does not. Our anticipated happiness is founded on no delusion — is no love-dream from which we must wake in the first year of our marriage.

Some of the worst (in the sense of technically inept) love letters are the most famous, and by the biggest hitters. The so-called 'Immortal Beloved' letters were unsent letters found among Beethoven's papers after his death. Their intended recipient is thought to have been Antonie Brentano, the wife of a merchant from Frankfurt. Reading them, you're relieved for her that Beethoven ran out of stamps.

Good morning, on 7 July

Even in bed my ideas yearn towards you, my Immortal Beloved, here and there joyfully, then again sadly, awaiting from Fate, whether it will listen to us. I can only live, either altogether with you or not at all. Yes, I have determined to wander about for so long far away, until I can fly into your arms and call myself quite at home with you, can send my soul enveloped by yours into the realm of spirits — yes, I regret, it must be. You will get over it all the more as you know my faithfulness to you; never another one can own my heart, never — never!...

What longing in tears for you — You — my Life — my All — farewell. Oh, go on loving me — never doubt the faithfullest heart

Of your beloved
L
Ever thine.
Ever mine.
Ever ours.

Why is this bad? Because it's so... thunderous. The language is empty and clichéd. It aspires to *appassionata* but might have been written by a machine.

Still, it could be worse. It could be as formulaic

as another anthology stalwart, the playwright William Congreve's letter to Arabella Hunt, a lutenist at court who had been married to a man called James Howard but filed for annulment after six months on the grounds that he was really a cross-dressing widow called Amy Poulter. (Hunt claimed that Howard/Poulter was a hermaphrodite, but a crack team of midwives examined him/her and decided he/she was biologically female.)

Dear Madam

Not believe that I love you? You cannot pretend to be so incredulous. If you do not believe my tongue, consult my eyes, consult your own. You will find by yours that they have charms; by mine that I have a heart which feels them. Recall to mind what happened last night. That at least was a lover's kiss. Its eagerness, its fierceness, its warmth, expressed the god its parent. But oh! Its sweetness, and its melting softness expressed him more. With trembling in my limbs, and fevers in my soul, I ravish'd it. Convulsions, pantings, murmurings shew'd the mighty disorder within me: the mighty disorder increased by it…

But Love, almighty Love, seems in a moment to have removed me to a prodigious distance from every object but you alone. In the midst of crowds I remain in solitude…

The scene of the world's great stage seems suddenly and sadly chang'd. Unlovely objects are all around me, excepting thee; the charms of all the world appear to be translated to thee. Thus in this sad, but oh, too pleasing state! my soul can fix upon nothing but thee; thee it contemplates, admires, adores, nay depends on, trusts on you alone.

Congreve's effort has the virtue of competence, even if its erotic flourishes are rather forced. But what about Nelson's lacklustre letters to fascinating, chameleonic Emma Hamilton, the blacksmith's daughter turned diplomat's wife who became his lover in 1798? On the basis of a single line – 'Nelson's Alpha and Omega is Emma!' – Nelson's love letters have been acclaimed. But it's all downhill from there. To wit:

I can neither Eat or Sleep for thinking of You my dearest love, I never touch even pudding You know the reason.

Well, she might, but we don't. For what reason is Nelson skipping cheesecake? Heartburn? Flatulence? Has Emma been teasing him about his flabby bottom?

Freud, meanwhile, would not have taxed himself interpreting this:

In one of my dreams I thought I was at a large Table You was not present, Sitting between a princess who I detest and another. They both tried to Seduce Me and the first wanted to take those liberties with Me which no Woman in this World but Yourself ever did. The consequence was I knocked her down and in the moment of bustle You came in and taking Me in Your embrace wispered I love nothing but You My Nelson. I kissed You fervently And we enjoy'd the height of love.

Was ever an erotic dream – at least, I assume that's what it is – rendered so flatly?

If what I was saying earlier about 'anything going' in love letters is true – that they are a hallowed space where you should be allowed to be whatever you want: angry, jealous and afraid as well as smug and self-satisfied – shouldn't they be judged less harshly than 'normal' letters? Should they even be judged at all? Remember Heloise's remark to Abelard: 'In spite of all our misfortunes you may be what you please in your letter.'

Keats was what he pleased in his letters to Fanny Brawne – and suffered for it. I've touched already on the way the publication of 37 of his letters to Fanny in February 1878 caused outrage and, in some quarters, the total collapse of his reputation.

Partly this was because their publisher H Buxton Forman was held to have infringed Keats's privacy. Other objections had to do with what the letters revealed about Keats, personally and aesthetically.

Matthew Arnold regarded the letters as those 'of a youth ill brought up, without the training which teaches us that we must put some constraint upon our feelings and upon the expression of them'. Dismayed by the letters' emotional gushiness, he felt that 'we cannot but look for signs in [Keats] of something more than sensuousness, for signs of character and virtue.'

Algernon Swinburne, in an entry for the 1882 (ie post-Fanny) edition of the *Encyclopaedia Britannica*, was able to get away with calling Keats 'a vapid and effeminate rhymester in the sickly stage of whelphood' and thought his love letters 'ought never to have been written... [E]ven a manly sort of boy, in his love-making or in his suffering, will not howl and snivel after such a lamentable fashion'.

Hang on, you want to say. These are love letters! They weren't written for public consumption. On the contrary, Keats was so keen to keep Fanny's letters to him private that he requested they be buried with him, which they were.

In any case, are they so bad? (We read them differently today, of course, now that men are expected to be gushy and declarative.)

25 College Street

My dearest Girl,

This moment I have set myself to copy some verses out fair. I cannot proceed with any degree of content. I must write you a line or two and see if that will assist in dismissing you from my Mind for ever so short a time. Upon my Soul I can think of nothing else... My love has made me selfish. I cannot exist without you — I am forgetful of every thing but seeing you again — my Life seems to stop there — I see no further. You have absorb'd me. I have a sensation at the present moment as though I was dissolving — I should be exquisitely miserable without the hope of soon seeing you. I should be afraid to separate myself far from you. My sweet Fanny, will your heart never change? My love, will it?...

I have been astonished that Men could die Martyrs for religion — I have shudde'd at it — I shudder no more — I could be martyr'd for my Religion — Love is my religion — I could die for that — I could die for you. My Creed is Love and you are its only tenet — You have ravish'd me away by a Power I cannot resist: and yet I could resist till I saw you; and even since I have seen you I have

endeavoured often 'to reason against the reasons of
my Love'. I can do that no more — the pain would
be too great — My Love is selfish — I cannot breathe
without you.

Yours for ever
John Keats

That's all right, isn't it? What's wrong with that? It's a bit formulaic (love is my religion, blah blah), but heartfelt.

Actually, Fanny got the nastiest notices on publication. Reviewing the collection, Richard Le Gallienne echoed the snobby, misogynist consensus when he wrote:

It is certainly a particularly ironical paradox that
the lady irritatingly associated with [Keats's]
name should be the least congruous of all the many
commonplace women transfigured by the genius
they could not understand, and the love of which
they were not worthy... Fame, that loves to humour
its poets, has consented to glorify the names of many
unimportant poor relations of genius, but there has
never been a more significant name upon its lips
than the name of Fanny Brawne... One writes so,
remembering... the tortures to which she subjected a
noble spirit with her dancing-class coquetries.

Death Becomes Us

On February 22 1815, after a pregnancy dominated by illness, Mary Shelley gave birth to a two-month-premature baby girl. On March 6, she wrote this heartbreaking letter to her husband Percy's friend Thomas Jefferson Hogg, whom she'd befriended herself during Percy's bouts of philandering:

> *My dearest Hogg my baby is dead — will you come to see me as soon as you can. I wish to see you — It was perfectly well when I went to bed — I awoke in the night to give it suck it appeared to be sleeping so quietly that I would not awake it. It was dead then, but we did not find that out till morning — from its appearance it evidently died of convulsions — Will you come — you are so calm a creature & Shelley is afraid of a fever from the milk — for I am no longer a mother now.*

Mary Shelley's own mother Mary Wollestonecraft had died giving birth to her in August 1797. When the placenta failed to be delivered, it was removed surgically using the crude methods of the time. The result was an acute infection and she died on September 10. William Godwin wrote to his friend, the writer Thomas Holcroft:

> *My wife is now dead. She died this morning at eight o'clock. She grew worse before your letter arrived...*
>
> *I firmly believe that there does not exist her equal in the world. I know from experience we were formed to make each other happy. I have not the least expectation that I can now ever know happiness again.*
>
> *When you come to town, look at me, and talk to me, but do not — if you can help it — exhort me, or console me.*

What is it with death and letters? The scene in Anthony Minghella's film of *The English Patient* that makes susceptible viewers cry (and less susceptible ones snort) is the one towards the end where a badly injured Kristin Scott Thomas languishes in the Cave of Swimmers while Ralph Fiennes trudges across the desert to get help. *You* remember.

Kristin uses the time to write Ralph a letter in

the back of his copy of Herodotus's *Histories*, a lyrical farewell – 'We die, we die rich with lovers and tribes...' – which we hear as voiceover just as Ralph is discovering her corpse and carrying it out into the sunlight. It concludes: 'The lamp has gone out, and I'm writing in the darkness.'

I like the scene against my better judgement because it makes explicit a connection between writing and death, the place where all stories end. It highlights, too, the desperate, often beautiful frailty proper letters radiate, one which becomes more apparent as a correspondence is impeded by the obstacles life puts in its way: disease, dementia, decrepitude.

As we have seen, soldiers' letters are full of the awful pathos of untimely death, all the worse for it being expected, part of the package. But to know that it was imminent, and that a letter was your only means of saying goodbye to those you loved... Kristin's letter reminds me of the letter written by Sir Thomas More to his daughter Margaret Roper on July 5, 1535, the night before his execution. He too was writing in the darkness, imprisoned in the Tower of London. As he had no pen, he used a tiny piece of charcoal.

Our Lord bless you good daughter and your good husband and your little boy and all yours and all my children and all my godchildren and all our friends...

I cumber you good Margaret much, but I would be
sorry, if it should be any longer than tomorrow, for
it is St Thomas's Eve, and the utas of St Peter and
therefore tomorrow long I to go to God, it were a day
very meet and convenient for me. I never liked your
manner toward me better than when you kissed me
last for I love when daughterly love and dear charity
hath no leisure to look to worldly courtesy.

Farewell my dear child, and pray for me, and I
shall for you and all your friends that we may merrily
meet in heaven. I thank you for your great cost.

(More was, of course, beheaded, and his head
displayed on a pike on London Bridge. Margaret
was so appalled that she bribed the man whose job
it was to dispose of the head to give it to her instead.
She preserved it by pickling it in spices.)

We write, as I said before, to assert ourselves
and keep death at bay. The scene in *The English*
Patient is sad because Kristin's letter has failed to
keep her alive when that is what we wanted it to do.
We want letters to have talismanic properties. But
at a certain point we have to accept that they don't,
at least not always, and the writer to admit that the
physical effort of putting pen to paper has become
too much.

Try this, a letter from essayist William Hazlitt to

the Scottish judge and literary critic Francis Jeffrey, written in September 1830:

> *Dear Sir,*
>
> *I am dying; can you send me £10 & so consummate your many kindnesses to me?*
>
> *W Hazlitt*

Or (much better – in fact one of the greatest last letters of them all) Keats's last surviving letter, written from Rome to his best friend Charles Armitage Brown on November 30, 1820.

> *My dear Brown,*
>
> *'Tis the most difficult thing in the world to me to write a letter. My stomach continues so bad, that I feel it worse on opening any book, – yet I am much better than I was in Quarantine. Then I am afraid to encounter the proing and conning of any thing interesting to me in England. I have an habitual feeling of my real life having past, and that I am leading a posthumous existence. God knows how it would have been – but it appears to me – however, I will not speak of that subject. I must have been at Bedhampton nearly at the time you were writing to me from Chichester – how unfortunate – and to*

pass on the river too! There was my star predominant! I cannot answer any thing in your letter, which followed me from Naples to Rome, because I am afraid to look it over again. I am so weak (in mind) that I cannot bear the sight of any hand writing of a friend I love so much as I do you. Yet I ride the little horse, — and, at my worst, even in Quarantine, summoned up more puns, in a sort of desperation, in one week than in any year of my life. There is one thought enough to kill me — I have been well, healthy, alert &c, walking with her — and now — the knowledge of contrast, feeling for light and shade, all that information (primitive sense) necessary for a poem are great enemies to the recovery of the stomach. There, you rogue, I put you to the torture, — but you must bring your philosophy to bear — as I do mine, really — or how should I be able to live?...

If I recover, I will do all in my power to correct the mistakes made during sickness; and if I should not, all my faults will be forgiven. I shall write to xxxx [name deleted by Brown] tomorrow, or next day. I will write to xxxx in the middle of next week... Remember me to all friends, and tell xxxx I should not have left London without taking leave of him, but from being so low in body and mind. Write to George as soon as you receive this, and tell

*him how I am, as far as you can guess; — and also
a note to my sister — who walks about my imagination like a ghost — she is so like Tom. I can scarcely
bid you good bye even in a letter. I always made an
awkward bow.*

*God bless you !
John Keats*

Keats was only 24 when he died. Imagine! He succumbed to tuberculosis shortly after the publication of his third and final book, *Lamia, Isabella, The Eve of St Agnes and Other Poems.* Though regarded now as containing some of the greatest poems ever written, its contemporary reception was no kinder than that accorded his previous books. So Keats died believing himself to be a failure: "'If I should die," said I to myself, "I have left no immortal work behind me — nothing to make my friends proud of my memory — but I have lov'd the principle of beauty in all things, and if I had had time I would have made myself remember'd.'"

By the summer of 1820 he knew that he was terminally ill. Joseph Severn, who had accompanied Keats to Rome, announced his death to Charles Armitage Brown in a letter dated February 27, 1821:

My dear Brown,

He is gone – he died with the most perfect ease – he seemed to go to sleep. On the 23rd, about 4, the approaches of death came on. "Severn-I-lift me up-I am dying-I shall die easy-don't be frightened-be firm, and thank God it has come!" I lifted him up in my arms. The phlegm seemed boiling in his throat, and increased until 11, when he gradually sunk into death – so quiet-that I still thought he slept. I cannot say now – I am broken down from four nights' watching, and no sleep since, and my poor Keats gone. Three days since, the body was opened; the lungs were completely gone. The Doctors could not conceive by what means he had lived these two months. I followed his poor body to the grave on Monday, with many English. They take such care of me here--that I must, else, have gone into a fever. I am better now--but still quite disabled.

The Police have been. The furniture, the walls, the floor, every thing must be destroyed by order of the law. But this is well looked to by Dr C.

The letters I put into the coffin with my own hand.

I must leave off.

J. S.

This goes by the first post. Some of my kind friends would have written else. I will try to write you every thing next post; or the Doctor will.

They had a mask--and hand and foot done--
I cannot get on--

Keats had written in a sonnet of his fears 'that I may cease to be/Before my pen has gleaned my teeming brain'. What if he had lived longer? What if he had kept writing and died in his sixties or seventies? Would his brain have continued to teem?

Neurologists agree that important cognitive changes occur in late middle age. Goals narrow. Forgetfulness and absentmindedness increase so that it becomes harder to inhibit what's irrelevant and retrieve what's important. Speech becomes slower, the right words harder to find.

But there are benefits, nebulous though they may sound. Wisdom – that is, hoarded insight into human nature and social relationships – increases; ditto interest in health, both your own and other people's. Little wonder, then, that these qualities dominate in letters by the elderly; also glibness and eccentricity.

After being diagnosed with heart disease, the novelist Wilkie Collins set out his rules for living to his friend Holman Hunt in a jaunty 'prescription' letter dated October 8, 1885:

> *The three rules of life that I find the right ones, in the matter of health, are:*

> *As much fresh air as possible (I don't get as much as I ought)*

> *Eat well — eat light and nourishing food, eggs, birds, fish, sweetmeats — no heavy chops or joints. And find out the wine that agrees with you, and don't be afraid of it. (Here I set an excellent example!)*

> *Empty your mind of your work before you go to bed — and don't let the work get in again until after break- fast the next morning. (This is a serious struggle — many defeats must be encountered — but the victory may be won at last, as I can personally certify.)*

John Ruskin battled madness for most of his life. After his first attack in June 1878 when he was 59, he wrote to Thomas Carlyle — an account of his hallucinations which has about it an awful and not entirely convincing jocularity:

> *I have not written to you, because my illness broke me all to pieces, and every little bit has a*

different thing to say, — which makes it difficult in the extreme to write to any one whom one wants to tell things to, just as they are, and who cares very truly whether they are right or wrong. It was utterly wonderful to find I could go so heartily & headily mad; for you know I had been priding myself on my peculiar sanity! And it was more wonderful yet to find the madness made up into things so dreadful, out of things so trivial. One of the most provoking and disagreeable of the spectres was developed out of the firelight on my mahogany bedpost — and my fate, for all futurity, seemed continually to turn on the humour of dark personages who were materially nothing but the stains of damp on the ceiling.

John Clare kept all the letters he received and stitched them into hand-made books. After a brief period of celebrity in the early 1820s as 'the Northamptonshire Peasant Poet' his star waned and in July 1837, after suffering a mental breakdown, he checked himself into a private asylum in Epping Forest. In 1841 he absconded, intending to visit his childhood sweetheart: he didn't realise she was dead. His personal doctor, Fenwick Skrimshire, signed his admission papers to a different, public asylum in Northampton. To the question 'Was the insanity preceded by any severe or long-continued mental emotion or exertion?', Skrimshire replied: 'After years addicted to Poetical prosing.'

In the asylum Clare wrote fragmentary poems about, and (unsent) love letters to, local women, some of which use a code involving the removal of all vowels and the letter y. One of them, decoded, looks like this:

> *My Dearest Mary Collingwood,*
>
> *I am nearly worn out and want to hear from you – Nobody will own me or have me at any price and what have I done – Do you know what you are in my Debt – kisses for ten years and longer still and longer than that – when people make such mistakes as to call me God's bastard and whores pay me by shutting me up from God's people out of the way of common sense and then take my head off because they can't find me – it out-Herods Herod.*

We have no idea who Mary Collingwood was. And as Clare's biographer Jonathan Bate observes, 'even once one has broken the code, it is impossible to decipher the sub-text'. The letter functions only as a glimpse 'inside [Clare's] head during a phase of derangement'.

Clare's most famous poem is a rapt meditation on identity and eternity: 'I am – yet what I am, none cares or knows...' His asylum letters follow this theme into a fog of unknowing, a place where he has lost all sense of home and family and self. By the time he wrote the letter below, to a well-meaning Westminster gentleman called James Hipkins, he was spending the bulk of his days on a bench in the asylum gardens, chewing tobacco.

March 8, 1860

Dear Sir,

I am in a Madhouse & quite forget your Name or who you are you must excuse me for I have nothing to commu[n]icate or tell of & why I am shut up I dont know I have nothing to say so I conclude.

yours respectfully
John Clare

William Cowper is an unusual case in that he always writes as if he were old, even when he isn't. When he *was* actually old, his preoccupations weren't markedly different from thirty years before; and remarkably, he retained the ability to write beautiful sentences to the end, though he is boringly obsessed with his own fitfulness as a correspondent. This letter to the Reverend John Newton was written a couple of years before his death – though you would think it was written two *weeks* before:

July 29, 1798

Dear Sir,

Few letters have passed between us, and I was never so incapable of writing as now, nor ever so destitute of a subject. It is long since I received your last, to which I have as yet returned no answer; nor is it possible that, though I write, I should even now reply to it…

I once little thought to see such days as these, for almost in the moment when they found me there was not a man in the world who seemed to himself to have less reason to expect them. This you know; and what can I say of myself that you do not know?

The End of the End

It's hard to make sense of deterioration and death. But letter-writing can help us find meaning in changing circumstances. If we set our minds to a low frequency, reduce the sounds of the world to an ambient hum and pick up a pen, wondrous things can be achieved. Letter-writing isn't nostalgic escapism. It's about re-evaluating yourself and the quality of your connectedness.

But how does that work, exactly?

Part 3

A Cure for Timesickness

Slow the World Down, One Letter at a Time

To make the point that, had email existed, writers like Coleridge and Emerson would have used it is, well, pointless. They didn't have email; they couldn't use it. As a result they wrote (and thought, and felt, and existed) differently because they had a different concept of space and time.

Handwritten letters of the length they usually wrote took an age to produce and were a function of an isolation it's almost impossible for us to understand. On top of which, the postal system was a bit hit-and-miss so you wrote half-assuming your letter would never be received, aware that *if* it wasn't received and you didn't send a swift follow-up your correspondent would worry you were dead. 'I am concerned at not hearing from you,' Emerson tells Carlyle in April 1836. 'Speak to me out of the wide silence.'

Things haven't been *really* slow for a while. But Douglas Coupland traces the unruly fastness of contemporary culture to 2003: the year he first felt the texture of daily life in Western media-driven societies start to warp. By now, of course, it's bent thoroughly out of shape: 'There's no more tolerance for waiting of any sort,' writes Coupland in his lovely little book about Marshall McLuhan, *You Know Nothing of My Work!*. 'We want all the facts and we want them *now*. To go without email for 48 hours can trigger a meltdown. You can't slow down, even once, ever, without becoming irrelevant.'

Claude Debussy's sister described him at the age of eight as spending 'whole days sitting on a chair thinking, no-one knew of what'. If a child did that now, he'd be diagnosed with ADD.

In Coupland's eyes we have become 'timesick'. And as communications media increasingly become technological extensions of our senses, no-one is working too hard to find a cure. We *need* the speed. Some people even like it. And if you don't – tough: over the next 50 years, say neuroscientists, our thought processes will accelerate exponentially.

This isn't a good thing, because as literacy guru Maryanne Wolf explains in her book *Proust and the Squid*, the need for delay is built into our brains. 'Delay neurons' regulate signal transmission. The delay they create lasts only milliseconds, but it allows 'sequence and order in our apprehension of reality'. Speed the world up too much and our relationship to it is thrown out of kilter.

As for our relationship to language, Wolf isn't hopeful: 'Will the present generation become so accustomed to immediate access to on-screen information that the range of attentional, inferential, and reflective capacities in the present reading brain will become less developed?'

It's one of those questions that supplies its own answer.

Perhaps the only way to regain the habit of long-form letter-writing is to slow my world down; follow the path Carl Honoré mapped out in his book *In Praise of Slow*. Honoré's interest in slow movements — the best known of which is the Slow Food organisation, founded in Italy in 1986 by Carlo Petrini — was sparked when he was browsing in an airport bookshop and found, to his distress, a book titled *The One-Minute Bedtime Story*.

'Slow reading', one of the strategies he recommends, has long had charismatic advocates like Sven Birkerts — the author, way back in 1994, of a brilliant book called *The Gutenberg Elegies: The Fate of Reading in an Electronic Age*. Even then, when the internet was for nerds only and mobile phones drew chuckles in restaurants, Birkerts noticed that 'a finely filamented electronic scrim has slipped between ourselves and the so-called "outside world"' and warned against the 'ersatz security of a vast lateral connectedness'.

Birkerts is fair-minded enough to appreciate the gains of what he quaintly calls 'electronic post-modernity', especially its fostering of a global 'big picture'. But in the debit ledger are 'a fragmented sense of time' and growing impatience with the 'so-called duration experience, that depth phenomenon we associate with reverie'.

'Reading, because we control it, is adaptable to our needs and rhythms,' Birkerts writes. 'We are free to indulge our subjective associative impulse; the term I coin for this is deep reading: the slow and meditative possession of a book.'

A necessary complement of reverie-driven slow reading must be slow writing. By which I don't mean the kind of angsty lucubration sufferers from writer's block will recognise, or even all writing produced anywhere as a consequence of cognitive deceleration (although in my utopia *all* writing is a consequence of cognitive deceleration). I mean a wholesale creative re-engagement with word-formation at the level of the graphic.

Basically: it's all about handwriting.

When I held my school letters in my hand and felt all wobbly and emotional, to which aspect of their materiality was I responding? The fading ink? The way the cheap brown envelope had been ripped open?

Or was it the sight of my nine-year-old self's clumpy scrawl?

Handwriting is richly, complicatedly evocative. It takes the letter-as-stand-in-for-person thing to a different level. Thomas Carlyle, writing to Ralph Waldo Emerson in 1870, 36 years after their correspondence began, drives this idea home when he calls it 'quite strangely interesting to see face to face my old Emerson again, not a feature of him changed, whom I have known all the best part of my life'.

Because it is unique to a person, handwriting is a physical token of identity and authenticity. This is why signatures on legal documents and works of art have historically been so important: they represent the presence of a particular person in a particular place at a particular moment. To reproduce someone's signature is to be guilty of forgery. But isn't forgery a meaningless, antique notion in a digital culture where there is no longer such a thing as an 'original'?

For the philosopher and critic Walter Benjamin, an original work of art had an 'aura' reflecting its singularity, its 'presence in time and space', its 'unique existence at the place where it happens to be'. Reproduced artworks lack this aura, says Benjamin, though he didn't live long enough to witness the sort of art where the reproduction is the whole point: the industrial screenprinting of Andy Warhol, or indeed the German conceptual artist Timm Ulrichs' arch 1967 reprograph of 100 (de)generations of the title page of Benjamin's essay 'The Work of Art in the Age of Mechanical Reproduction'.

Is this why letters feel different? Because they have a version of this aura?

The word 'authentic' has become synonymous with 'traditional' in a way that makes it easy to sneer at. But sometimes it matters that things are authentic. Around ten years ago, the Anne Frank Museum made two sets of facsimile copies of Anne's six notebooks to protect the originals from damage. Recognising that it was vital to preserve the notebooks' aura, they spent a fortune ensuring the copies were perfect right down to the postmarked stamps and spots of rust on the clasp.

Why all that effort? Because nothing about Anne Frank can be allowed to be counterfeit: that way lies Holocaust denial. Her diary *is* the Holocaust. What the curators evidently hoped is that the copies would somehow retain the aura of the originals in a circle-squaring act of philosophical optimism none of us is in a position to criticise.

But now the idea of letters as a trope of authenticity is abused by corporate marketing. (Every bottle of Aussie shampoo invites you to write to Aussie: 'Questions? Give us a ring, send us an email or even put pen to paper. We like getting letters, no-one does it these days and it makes us feel special.' Never mind that Aussie is actually owned by Procter & Gamble.)

Authentic Friendships

Epistolary friendships are underwritten by this authenticity. The best evolve organically, taking their cue from the rhythm of the correspondence.

Epistolary friendships focus on the interior self – on a person's individual ways of thinking and feeling and seeing. This isn't always a straightforward business. Letters can be extraordinarily candid and personal. But anyone who has ever written one knows that they can also be slippery and disingenuous. (Arguably, the best letters are both at once.) Epistolary friendships can be so intense, so satisfying, that when the correspondents actually meet it's a crushing disappointment.

Nowadays, of course, you can conduct epistolary friendships online. Everyone knows someone who met their partner on Twitter or used Facebook to convene a gathering of old schoolfriends. But there is something missing from this ethertalk; maybe even *every*thing.

On the train on the way back from my mother's flat, marvelling at how far from speech perfected my letters home pitched themselves, I thought about Charles Lamb, something I hadn't done since I was an undergraduate twenty-odd years ago.

Lamb is the English poet and essayist best loved for the *Tales from Shakespeare* he co-wrote with his sister Mary and his *Essays of Elia*, pseudonymous conversational ruminations – Elia was the name of an Italian clerk he worked with at South Sea House – which appeared in *The London Magazine* between 1820 and 1825.

Charles and Mary both endured fragile mental health. Among Charles's most moving letters are those written to his old schoolfriend Samuel Taylor Coleridge charting its giddy ups and frequent, devastating downs.

In 1796, Mary suffered a breakdown and killed their mother with a kitchen knife. Charles negotiated her release from the asylum to which she was subsequently sent by offering to be her guardian. But in the period between her committal and return home he wrote some powerful, clarifying letters to Coleridge expressing his state of mind.

One little incident may serve to make you under-stand my way of managing my mind [he wrote].

Within a day or two after the fatal one, we dressed for dinner a tongue which we had salted for some weeks in the house. As I sat down, a feeling like remorse struck me: this poor tongue Mary got for me, and can I partake of it now, when she is far away? A thought occurred and relieved me; if I give in to this way of feeling, there is not a chair, a room, an object in our rooms, that will not awaken the keenest griefs; I must rise above such weaknesses. I hope this was not want of true feeling.

I mention these things because I hate concealment, and love to give a faithful journal of what passes within me.

The reader feels privileged, witnessing someone 'working through' grief so eloquently. That this is a letter and not a diary entry is significant. A diary is private, a receptacle for confidences. This letter, on the other hand, deals explicitly with what it's acceptable (and bearable) to feel (and say). It is helping to regulate emotion, to keep the brain well tempered.

Reading Charles's letters to his old friend, you are struck by how vital the correspondence was to him, how much it sustained and soothed him. 'I had put my letter into the post rather hastily, not expecting to have to acknowledge another from you so soon,' he writes on December 10, 1796. 'This morning's present has made me alive again.' The little fits of self-loathing are neutralised by common sense, as in one lengthy letter dated January 10, 1797: 'My letter is full of nothingness. I talk of nothing. But I must talk. I love to write to you. I take a pride in it. It makes me think less meanly of myself. It makes me think myself not totally disconnected from the better part of mankind.'

The correspondence was important because of what the letters *contained*, but also because the letters are objects whose solidity compensates, very effectively, for their author's absence. When Lamb tells Wordsworth (March 20, 1822), 'A letter from you is very grateful; I have not seen a Kendal postmark so long', this metonymy is made explicit; though not as explicit as when, to give other examples, Keats implores Fanny Brawne to 'make [your letter] rich as a draught of poppies to intoxicate me – write the softest words and kiss them that I may at least touch my lips where yours have been', or Emily Dickinson writes to Elizabeth Holland, 'I kiss my paper here for you... would it were cheeks instead'.

As I said earlier, letters shape and define lives. This is why great correspondences like the 40-odd-year transatlantic one between Carlyle and Emerson fascinate and surprise us.

Emerson was pompous, egomaniacal and given to abstruse waffle. Carlyle was a grumpy old Calvinist locked in an unhappy marriage. But if what you want is rapt rumination on nature, consciousness, materialism and free will (with a lot of publishing gossip thrown in), look no further than their extraordinary letters to each other.

Emerson and Carlyle's bumpy friendship was almost entirely epistolary, though it took a meeting to bring it to fruition. In 1833, Emerson left Boston to take a tour of Europe. He stopped off to visit the Carlyles at their cottage in the Scottish town of Craigenputtock.

They got on well. Emerson found Carlyle 'tall and gaunt, with a cliff-like brow, self-possessed and holding his extraordinary powers of conversation in easy command'. But nine months would pass before Emerson wrote the first of his famous letters to his host, a letter that begins with one of the all-time great excuses for not having written sooner:

There are some purposes we delay long to execute simply because we have them more at heart than

others, and such a one has been for many weeks, I may
say months, my design of writing you an epistle.

He follows this with a searing, borderline rude
critique of Carlyle's philosophical satire *Sartor*
Resartus which concludes:

> *If any word in my letter should provoke you to a*
> *reply, I shall rejoice in my sauciness.*

Carlyle does reply, almost biting his tongue off
with the effort of not writing 'You are seven years
younger than me and not yet published – so sod off':

> *With regard to style and so forth, what you call*
> *your 'saucy' objections are not only most intelligible*
> *to me, but welcome and instructive.*

There was a minimum gap of two months
between letters: that was how long it took for them
to cross the Atlantic. But the fact that they were
able to communicate at all was amazing, thought
Carlyle:

> *On the whole, as the Atlantic is so broad and deep,*
> *ought we not rather to esteem it a beneficent miracle*
> *that messages can arrive at all; that a little slip of*

paper will skim over all these weltering floods, and other inextricable confusions, and come at last, in the hand of the Twopenny Postman, safe to your lurking-place, like green leaf in the bill of Noah's Dove?

Over the years Emerson shares with Carlyle details of his marriage, the deaths of his brothers, the birth of his son and the publication of his first book, *Nature*. The tension between the elevated tone and intimate subject matter – and between the pair's temperaments and viewpoints – is fascinating. Emerson effectively became Carlyle's American agent and editor, and much of the correspondence deals with publishing business, what Carlyle called their 'bibliopoly'. The money he made from American sales kept Carlyle afloat, and in 1844, upon receipt of £36 in royalties, Carlyle remarks to Emerson: 'America, I think, is like an amiable family tea-pot; you think it is all out long since, and lo, the valuable implement yields you another cup, and another!'

Carlyle struggles to complete his history of the French Revolution. Emerson begs Carlyle to come to America and lecture; Carlyle bats the offer away. Sometimes Emerson's windy abstraction irritates Carlyle and he mocks: 'I do again desiderate some concretion of these beautifulabstracta.' Emerson is enthusiastic about people and new projects. Carlyle hates his work and whinges constantly.

By 1850, a few years after Emerson's second visit to the Carlyles ends in a happy visit to Stonehenge but also a huge row about Cromwell's abilities as a leader, Carlyle can see 'well enough what a great deep cleft divides us in our ways of practically looking at the world'.

Emerson fights for the abolition of slavery. Carlyle thinks that slavery might well be the only way to get lazy Irish people to work; that democracy is a foolish idea; and that what countries really need is strong, charismatic leadership by Great Men. Emerson disagrees and, moreover, dislikes Carlyle's creeping anti-Americanism: 'I have long ceased to apologise for or explain your savage sayings about American or other republics.'

During the 1850s the correspondence tails off. Emerson falls silent. Carlyle senses disapproval and tries to excuse himself: 'As if I could have *helped* growing to be, by aid of time and destiny, the grim Ishmaelite I am, and so shocking your serenity by my ferocities!'

Eventually Emerson does reply, and while there's a certain lack of engagement (and increasingly long gaps between letters) the old respect shines through.

Carlyle wrote his final letter to Emerson in April 1872. The letter praises John Ruskin before concluding:

> *Alas, alas, here is the end of the paper, dear Emerson; and I had still a whole wilderness of things to say. Write to me, or even do not write, and I will surely write again.*
>
> *I remain as ever Your Affectionate Friend,*
>
> *T. Carlyle*

Henry James got it right, in an 1883 review, that the Carlyle/Emerson letters would continue to be read by those 'even further removed from the occasion than ourselves and for whom possibly the vogue of Carlyle's published writings in his day will be to a certain degree a subject of wonder'.

Who reads Carlyle's work today apart from students of nineteenth-century history? Hardly anyone. But his letters transcend their time because, as James says, 'all his great merits come out in this form of expression, and his defects are not felt as defects, but only as striking characteristics and as tones in the picture'. These merits, which James itemises, can be seen as the merits all good letters should possess: 'Originality, nature, humour, imagination, freedom, the disposition to talk, the play of mood, the touch of confidence.'

Charles Lamb liked writing letters because it made him feel 'not totally disconnected from the better part of mankind'. But is the connectedness he had in mind the same as the connectedness I celebrated earlier today when I tweeted to my 139 followers: 'I really must take the sticker proclaiming "I Spent the Day with Thomas the Tank Engine" off my coat'?

Of course it isn't.

That's why I'm here now, sitting at the kitchen table, practising what I have been preaching. This moment is the culmination of all that I know and have thought about letters. The pen must become part of me again, part of my central nervous system.

I'm not trying to 'emulate the greats' and produce something of literary value, whatever that is. I just want it to be chatty and intimate on its own terms; to feel *considered* (that word again) and be a proxy for me.

It's 10.07pm and the children are asleep. A standard lamp behind my left shoulder casts the only light. In front of me is a sheet of Smythson's paper. In my right hand I am holding the Mont Blanc fountain pen my wife bought me about ten years ago.

The paper is now covered in my scrawl, and the pen's ink reservoir is almost empty.

As I sign my name a jolt of satisfaction shoots up my arm. And I am happy.

▓▓▓▓▓▓▓ Road
London
SE24 ▓▓

February 26th, 2012

Dear Jane,

You probably don't remember, but back
in was it October (?) you wrote me a wonderful
letter. I want to call it a condolence letter,
but it did so much more than condole and I've
meant ~~wanted~~ ever since to reply in a manner that felt
worthy — that acknowledged not just what you
wrote but the effort you put into writing it
when I know how much else you've got going
on. That it's taken me so long is faintly
shameful. I can only plead lack of perspective
— it vanishes after a death, as you know,
and so much has happened since the funeral,
events which demand their own letter and
will get one at some point.

    I remember you saying it took you
a long time to rid yourself of the image of
the moment of death. That has now receded
for me, thank God, and it's the background,

ambient details that haunt me, if that's not too strong a word: the ping of alarm bells, the rumble of trolley wheels on lino. Hospice life. The other day I was hoovering round the sofa when I suddenly remembered the electric recliner armchair beside her bed — the way the children, when they came up to Macclesfield to say goodbye for the last time, spent the whole afternoon playing with it, as if that had been the whole point of the trip.

I do feel very strongly that life is different now. The worst of it, apart from the obvious loss, is the way the death of a parent forces you to confront the abandonment of your children that your own death will entail, and your partner's death, and your siblings' deaths, and your friends' ... I'm lucky I suppose that it happened this way round.

A lot of what I'm feeling is just the first stirrings of midlife angst. I'm reading Josephine Tey's The Franchise Affair at the moment — a lovely Folio Society edition — and there's a bit where she talks about

3

the way 'childhood's attitude of something -
wonderful - tomorrow persisted subconsciously in
a man as long as it was capable of
realisation, and it was only after forty, when
it became unlikely of fulfilment, that it
obtruded itself into conscious thought; a
lost piece of childhood crying for attention'.
That's great, isn't it? If you have them, then
your children become your something - wonderful -
tomorrow. But it can be anything — a sporting
goal, a project. The hard bit about the
                                           states of mind
conscious/subconscious thing is that noticing ~~them~~,
eg 'I am happy' can lead you into overthinking
them, eg 'Why am I happy? When will I stop
being happy?'

       How long did it take you to delete your
mum's number from your contacts list? I
still haven't. Maybe in a few months' time.

       Are we seeing you soon? I think so.
I hope so.
            love,
                 John X

SELECT
BIBLIOGRAPHY

A Letter Book, by George Saintsbury (Bell, 1922)

A Writer at War: Letters & Diaries 1939-45 by Iris Murdoch, ed. Peter J Conradi (Short Books, 2010)

Byron: Selected Letters and Journals, ed. Peter Gunn (Penguin, 1972)

Epistolary Practices: Letter-Writing in America Before Telecommunications, by William Merrill Decker (University of North Carolina Press, 1998)

Flourishing: Letters 1928-1946 by Isaiah Berlin, ed. Henry Hardy (Chatto & Windus, 2004)

Jane Austen's Letters, ed. Deirdre Le Faye (OUP, 1994)

Letters to Children, ed. Eva G Connor (Macmillan, 1938)

Letters to Pauline by Stendhal, ed. Adam Thirlwell (Hesperus, 2011)

Letters to a Young Poet by Rainer Maria Rilke, tr. and ed. Charlie Louth (Penguin, 2011)

Letter Writing as a Social Practice, by Lia Litosseliti and Jane Sunderland (John Benjamins, 2002)

Love Letters of Great Men, ed. Ursula Doyle (Macmillan, 2008)

Marshall McLuhan: You Know Nothing of My Work!, by Douglas Coupland (Atlas & Co, 2010)

Masters of the Post, by Duncan Campbell-Smith (Allen Lane, 2011)

Posting It: The Victorian Revolution in Letter Writing by Catherine J Golden (University Press of Florida, 2010)

Renaissance Eloquence, ed. James J Murphy (University of California Press, 1983)

Selected Letters by Julian Maclaren-Ross, ed. Paul Willetts (Black Spring Press, 2008)

Selected Letters by William Cowper (JM Dent, 1926)

Selected Letters by Wilfred Owen, ed. John Bell (OUP, 1986)

Selected Letters of Anton Chekhov, ed. Lillian Hellman (Hamish Hamilton, 1955)

Sign Here! Handwriting in the Age of New Media, eds. Sonja Neef, Jose Van Dijk, Eric Ketelaar (Amsterdam University Press, 2007)

Speaking For Themselves: The Personal Letters of Winston and Clementine Churchill, ed. Mary Soames (Doubleday, 1998)

So I Have Thought of You: The letters of Penelope Fitzgerald, ed. Terence Dooley (Fourth Estate, 2009)

The Christmas Letters: The Ultimate Collection of Round-Robin Letters, by Simon Hoggart (Atlantic, 2007)

The Faber Book of Letters, ed. Felix Pryor (Faber, 1988)

The Gutenberg Elegies: The Fate of Reading in an Electronic Age, by Sven Birkerts (Faber, 1994)

The Letters of Charles Lamb (E Moxon, 1837)

The Letters of Evelyn Waugh, ed. Mark Amory
(Weidenfeld & Nicolson, 1980)
The Oxford Book of Letters, ed. Frank and Anita Kermode
(OUP, 1995)
Cliff Tillotson, 'The Correspondence Between Ralph
Waldo Emerson and Thomas Carlyle', Institute of
World Culture (www.worldculture.org)

Thank You

Rebecca Nicolson, Aurea Carpenter and all at Short Books;
Antony Topping at Greene & Heaton; Katherine Stroud; Cathy
Newman; Martina Olusi; Mary Aldington and Anne Redshaw;
Brian O'Connell; Alex O'Connell; Peter Earl; Julia and David
Newman.

tempo@CB 5/14

mL

1-13